Caring for Aging Parents

Your Compassionate Guide to Regain Sanity, Reclaim Peace of Mind and Restore Life Balance to Avoid Burnout

Caring for Aging Parents

Your Compassionate Guide to Regain Sanity, Reclaim Peace of Mind and Restore Life Balance to Avoid Burnout

Elizabeth Roth

© **Copyright 2023 - All rights reserved.**

The content contained within this book may not be reproduced, duplicated or transmitted without direct written permission from the author or the publisher.

Under no circumstances will any blame or legal responsibility be held against the publisher, or author, for any damages, reparation, or monetary loss due to the information contained within this book, either directly or indirectly.

Legal Notice:

This book is copyright protected. It is only for personal use. You cannot amend, distribute, sell, use, quote or paraphrase any part, or the content within this book, without the consent of the author or publisher.

Disclaimer Notice:

Please note the information contained within this document is for educational and entertainment purposes only. All effort has been executed to present accurate, up to date, reliable, complete information. No warranties of any kind are declared or implied. Readers acknowledge that the author is not engaged in the rendering of legal, financial, medical or professional advice. The content within this book has been derived from various sources. Please consult a licensed professional before attempting any techniques outlined in this book.

By reading this document, the reader agrees that under no circumstances is the author responsible for any losses, direct or indirect, that are incurred as a result of the use of the information contained within this document, including, but not limited to, errors, omissions, or inaccuracies.

Contents

Prologue	1
Introduction	5
1. WHEN THE BRAIN AGES	**11**
Peer Spotlight: Heidi	11
Cognitive and Memory Impairments Associated With Aging	14
What Happens When Our Brain Ages?	15
Dementia	17
Memory Loss	19
What Is Normal Aging?	21
Chronic Conditions and Daily Life	24
2. HOME SAFETY AND MODIFICATION	**27**
Peer Spotlight: Alex	27
Assessing Your Home	29
Home Modification Suggestions	34
Interactive Element	38
3. NAVIGATING LEGAL AND FINANCIAL MATTERS	**41**
Peer Spotlight: Susan	41
A Guide to Estate Planning	43
Managing Aging Parents' Finances and Retirement Planning	46
Understanding Insurance Options	49
Planning and Choosing Insurance and Long-Term Care	52
Interactive Element	53

4. COMMUNICATING WITH SIBLINGS AND FAMILY MEMBERS — 57
- Peer Spotlight: Christine — 57
- Communicating With Elderly Parents — 60
- How to Communicate Effectively with Aging Parents — 63
- Communication Strategies Between Family Members — 65
- Dealing With Conflicts and Difficult Family Dynamics — 68
- Interactive Element — 71

5. HOW TO FIND AND MANAGE CAREGIVER RESOURCES — 75
- Peer Spotlight: Andrew — 75
- Types of Caregiver Resources — 78
- Managing the Costs — 84

6. EMOTIONAL SUPPORT FOR CAREGIVERS AND AGING PARENTS — 89
- Peer Spotlight: Isabella — 89
- Understanding the Emotional Impact of Aging and Caregiving — 91
- How to Reduce Isolation When Caregiving — 94
- How to Provide Emotional Support for Aging Parents — 97
- How to Find Emotional Support as a Caregiver — 99

7. BALANCING WORK AND CAREGIVER RESPONSIBILITIES — 102
- Peer Spotlight: Josh — 102
- Challenges We Face Balancing Work and Caregiving — 104
- Helpful Strategies — 107
- How to Communicate With Your Employer — 109

8. COPING STRATEGIES FOR STRESS AND
BURNOUT   112
Peer Spotlight: Emily and Sarah   112
Understanding Caregiver Stress and
Burnout   115
Why Are We Stressed and Burnt Out?   116
Self-Care Tips for Caregivers   119
How to Build Your Own Support System 121

9. PLANNING FOR THE FUTURE—TAKING
CARE OF YOURSELF AND YOUR
LOVED ONES   126
Peer Spotlight: David   126
The End   128
Dealing With Loss and Grief After
Caregiving   132
Coping With Guilt After Caregiving   134
Rebuilding Your Life After Caregiving   136

Afterword   141
Glossary   147
References   157

Prologue

The Diagnosis—March 2017

As I trudged down the hospital hallway toward the memory clinic, I caught myself in one of my discriminating, cynical thoughts: *If I had met her as an adult, I would not like her. She is too rigid, too anxious, too unaware of social norms, too inflexible to learn new things, and too afraid to accept new ideas. She is no fun. She is uptight and incapable of having a normal conversation without redirecting it to being about her.*

You may think me to be an ungrateful bitch, and I agree. After all, I am talking about my mother.

Once I arrived at the waiting room, I shook my head back to reality and squeezed in a final thought, my recent maxim: *I may not like her, but I have to help care for her; it's my responsibility.*

"Hey Bro," I said as I flopped down into the chair next to him.

"Yo!" he responded, setting his magazine onto his lap, "She is already in with the doctor."

We sat outside the exam room, waiting for our mother to finish with the geriatrician. We made light of the situation, as we usually do, mocking the people and things that surrounded us. I suppose you could call it a coping mechanism. In our family, turning to ridicule when in difficult situations is, well, cathartic.

The doctor finally invited us in to discuss her evaluation.

Our mom sat in the corner of the tiny room. Slumping forward into her poor posture, she fiddled with a little golf pencil with her crooked arthritic hands. She was eerily calm, and she wore a dissident, wry smirk. She had a naughty child-like demeanor. I suddenly found myself wanting to move mountains to remove my mother from this predicament. I felt like I was in my own daughter's principal's office, trying to bail her out for having justifiably broken school rules.

The doctor broke into my thoughts of pity, saying, "Five years ago, your mother's score was 28 of a possible 30 points on her Mini-Mental State Exam (MMSE). Today," he informed us, "her score is 12."

"Should we start thinking about moving her into some sort of assisted living or a retirement community?" I asked.

"No," he answered, "people in her state tend to react badly to a change in their environment."

My brother and I shared a catty look you would think was scripted for a scene from Mean Girls. We had been trying to get our mother to grow into the idea of downsizing for at least a year, and now this!

How could he undo our efforts?! She was down at least 40 pounds—she looked emaciated and frail, and she failed that mental state exam with flying colors.

Imagine that, I thought, *Mom used to be the nursing coordinator at an elder nursing home; her biggest fear has become her reality. She would be ashamed if she could see herself.*

Introduction

* * *

At the start of every school year, teachers were invited to hear a keynote speaker present about a given theme having to do with education. Over the years, we heard talks about learning disabilities, teaching with gender in mind, and bullying, to name a few.

In August 2015, I was 39 years old, a teacher for 14 of them, and the "start of the year" theme was life balance, but all the speaker talked about was the sandwich generation. At this moment, I thought, *why are teachers listening to something so outside the scope of education? This has absolutely zero to do with me and, certainly, nothing to do with gaining balance in our lives.* I had work to do and would much rather have been setting up my classroom and planning for the new year.

I learned that the sandwich generation refers to middle-aged people taking care of their aging parents and children simultaneously. Although I understood the concept and could sympathize with those living in this so-called sandwich, I still wondered what this had to do with me and the hundreds of educators in the auditorium. The presenter provided statistics about the elderly, nursing homes, all types of dementia, finances, baby boomers, and a little about life balance in relation to people caring for their aging parents.

I remember leaving that day informed about aging and financial planning but not a true grasp of what this had to do with teachers' work-life balance. Without a clue that six months later, I would be a member of this generation, and all of what I heard in that talk would be in clear focus. It is the reason why I wrote this book. If you are reading it, it is because you are on a journey that is inexplicable to those who are not on the same path. I didn't get "it."

It begins slowly. Your parents are fine. You notice things like the dents and dings on their car. They repeat themselves within the same conversation. It gets to the point that you are easily aggravated by their behavior. That aggravation is drowning in guilt, too, because you are trying to live your life. You are finally an adult and can do adult things. Whether it is growing your family, your career, or just finally having the life that you desire.

My mother was 74 when she started to exhibit signs that I now know were the onset of dementia. I had three older brothers that could act as gauges for our mother's behavioral changes and the apparent decline in autonomous ability. It was sad timing to witness this happening to her because my mother cared for her aging mother until she died at 96—merely four years prior to her own onset.

While my grandmother was in a nursing home until her

death, my mom's life was put on hold in many ways. One of the biggest was that she did not travel as she had always talked about doing after the four of us were no longer dependent. The unfortunate and regular health problems that my grandmother went through in the decade leading to her death would cripple my mother's opportunity to travel because she feared Grandma would need her. Sure, my brothers and I offered to take the reins while my mother went on a trip; she just wasn't able to—*it would be too stressful,* she would claim. Now, I get that.

For the past eight years, I have felt I had to put my life on hold because of my mother's deteriorating health. She has had countless moments of being on the verge of some health crisis or death. How can you go on a vacation when your parent(s) might need to be hospitalized or—and I am not being dramatic—they may die?

Thinking back, the signs were everywhere, but I just chalked it up to Mom being annoying again. She would send these weird passive-aggressive emails about how I never reached out to her. I would find myself talking with one of my brothers about what he sees and how she is just a miserable, depressed, and anxious person. Neither of us recognized what was happening to our mother. She was a lot sicker than we realized.

At one point, while she was still living independently in her own condo, we knew she was a menace on the road. We would try to address how we could have her license revoked, but we were at a loss; she was resistant and would practically throw a temper tantrum when it was brought up. As luck would have it, one day, my mother called me and said, "A nice policeman told me I will need to take a driving test if I want to maintain my license. But I hate tests, so I guess I will no longer drive." Even her storytelling had child-like components.

After her license was fortuitously taken away, other issues began to surface with her living an independent life. She still wanted to participate in her extra-curricular activities. Which in itself is very important, but without her car, she would need to find ways to get to her choir and line dancing practice. She would take the bus or get into a taxi and get lost. The sad part is that she didn't realize it. Although my mother never drank, her behavior was akin to her being drunk and confused.

A few years later, my father, who was also living in his own apartment independently, would begin to show his own signs of mental decline. With him, the signs were more apparent. After having witnessed my mother's demise, there were things I just knew. I knew how to be patient and not bark at him for being repetitive. I knew that it was time to take his car. I knew that certain safety issues needed to be addressed in his home. I knew what was happening to his mind. I knew some financial control needed to be transferred over to his kids. We had to move him out of his home and into assisted living—which really sucked because this happened during Covid. Since we had to go through that with my mother a few years prior, I also knew too well how to get that ball rolling.

Although the experience of caring for my father differed from that of my mother, there was a lot I learned from my mom that I could apply to my dad. In case you are wondering, at this point, my parents divorced when I was 9, and my brothers were 13, 18, and 20. I tell you this because I understand the roles we all play in our very unique families. The way things unfolded with caring for *my* aging parents may not be identical to yours, but there will be a lot of common ground.

As I write the introduction to this book, my mother is riddled with Alzheimer's and Lewy Body dementia, and it is going on four years that she does not recognize anyone or her surroundings. My oldest brother, 55, who suffered from schizophrenia for his whole life, died on September 17—my birthday. Needless to say, with our parents' states, this is something we chose not to share with them. Five months later, my father, at age 89, passed away. His death, February 25, 2023, occurred on the same day I boarded a cruise: that would not allow me to return home for his funeral in person. But arrangements were in place for this possibility.

The takeaway from the ongoing saga of my experience caring for my aging parents is that as much as this story has much tragedy, it also carries many lessons. Lessons about how we cope and plan. The fact is frustrations and moments of animosity, which so many of us face, are very real. One of the biggest lessons that I take from this is how we choose to respond to the shit show of caring for our parents is paramount to us coming out on top.

I write this book in hopes that it doesn't take you eight years to learn some of the things I have learned. Be it about our parents' aging brain and the signs of dementia; the safety measures that need to be put in place while they are still living on their own; financial measures and end-of-life planning; the difficulties that arise when communicating with siblings and family members; ideas around finding and managing caregivers; emotional support and life balance and responsibilities and avoiding burnout; and even planning for the future.

I have met some amazing humans during this journey. In order to keep this book relatable, my peers, Heidi, Alex, Susan, Christine, Andrew, Isabella, Emily and Sarah, as well as David, all agreed to allow their personal stories to grace the beginning of each chapter. Viewing this life through the eyes of those invested in it can offer hope, laughter, and guidance.

A huge part of my experience is the acceptance that I have one life to live, and the guilt that comes with living it while caring for my parents is normal but is not about others. I felt a lot of judgment from others, but I have learned that was my own construct. No one is in your shoes, and no one is actually judging how you navigate this tumultuous time.

As our parents age, there will be challenges and obstacles, but with the right information, you can still live a fulfilling life, and caring for others should not hold you back from doing the things you want. There is always a solution, and there is always help and support.

Chapter 1

When the Brain Ages

* * *

They may forget what you said, but they will never forget how you made them feel. —Maya Angelou

Peer Spotlight: Heidi

As mentioned in the introduction, I will begin each chapter with a personal story from one of my peers. These are people with whom I have crossed paths along my journey of coping with my aging parents. These are the amazing humans who I have had the pleasure of knowing by way of an unfortunate common bond.

We will begin with Heidi, who I met during the pandemic, in an online video support group. She was gracious enough to write her story for me to include in this book. I appreciate her support in writing even a small part of her caregiving saga so we can help others in the predicament of having to care for their aging loved ones.

I've spent my entire life believing I was the daughter, not the mother to my parents. But when my mother one day couldn't remember where she left her glasses, which were amusingly sitting on her head, I saw the roles had reversed. The revelation was bittersweet. I found myself on an unexpected path, morphing from a cherished daughter to a caregiver.

My father, already deep into his 80s, wasn't faring much better. The once vibrant and always reliable giant was starting to lose his strength, his memory lapses growing more frequent and severe. Each time my dad couldn't remember our old family dog's name or the story behind the dent in our vintage Buick, my heart ached.

The day came when, after a particularly bewildering conversation with my father about a lost remote control, I decided to turn to the vast wisdom of the internet. I made it my mission to learn everything I could about the aging brain. I've always been an insatiable reader, a genuine knowledge enthusiast, but this was different. This was personal.

The world of dementia and geriatric care was an endless sea of medical terminology and research papers I hadn't known existed. Words like neuroplasticity, cognitive reserve, and hippocampal atrophy became my new language—not exactly the kind of words I'd casually drop during Sunday dinner, but they were vital in understanding my parents' new reality.

I joined online support groups and connected with people going through similar situations. I found myself sharing tears with a woman from Nebraska caring for her Parkinson's-stricken husband and sharing laughs with a man from Maine, whose sense of humor remained untouched by his wife's Alzheimer's.

Throughout this journey, I gleaned wisdom, compassion, and a strong dose of reality from medical professionals and fellow caregivers. I discovered that my parents' aging was about so much more than fading memory; it was about the many intricate physiological and psychological factors at play. The conversations were often brutally honest, but they were also filled with advice and resources and shared laughter over unexpected joys and comic moments that emerged even in these difficult times.

I learned to be patient and to recognize the signs of confusion in my father's eyes before his frustration kicked in. I learned to laugh at the amusing moments, like when my mother jokingly referred to the glasses on her head as a stylish hat. I learned I wasn't alone, even on the toughest days when caregiving seemed like an insurmountable mountain.

In a strange way, I developed a deeper respect and love for my parents as I assisted them through this uncharted territory. They were still the same people who had raised me, loved me, and made me the person I am today. Their minds might be changing, but their spirits were as resilient as ever. Yes, the journey was bittersweet, but I found strength in the most unexpected places. And throughout it all, I was grateful for this opportunity to give back to those who had given me so much.

Through the story of Heidi, we can see how many families are impacted by a mental decline as their parents' age. Let's look a bit closer and how and why this happens.

Cognitive and Memory Impairments Associated With Aging

As I navigate through the middle years of my life, I've come to grasp the undeniable reality: aging reshapes us. It's not just about the physical transformation—the aching joints that once sprung me from bed each morning now meet each dawn with a slight groan. It's a whole lot more than that. It's about our minds, our brains, enduring their own unique evolution as we age.

As discussed in the introduction, my parents' brains were not immune to this complex process. I've seen certain abilities, like memory and spatial recognition, dwindle with time. It's a curious and intricate shift, and it leaves me wondering about the why and the how.

Why do these changes occur in our brains, the most complicated of all our organs? What are these alterations telling us about our aging selves? What does it mean for public health, especially with a rapidly aging population?

Today, I find myself part of the "sandwich generation", a term that couldn't feel more apt. It feels like I'm trapped in the middle, caring for my own family on one side and my aging mother on the other. Her Alzheimer's and dementia diagnosis weighs heavily on me. It's a relentless storm, leaving me emotionally ravaged, teetering on the brink of exhaustion.

What Happens When Our Brain Ages?

During our formative years, our brains are a hub of activity, forming more than a million new neural connections per second. By the age of 6, our brains have already grown to roughly 90% of the volume they'll have in adulthood (Columbia University, 2021).

Subsequently, as we enter our third and fourth decades of life, our brains begin to reduce in size, a process that accelerates after the age of sixty. This is akin to the appearance of wrinkles and the graying of our hair as we age. The physical alteration of our brains signals changes in our cognitive abilities as well.

I wanted to look at some common shifts that occur as we grow older.

Brain Mass

As she's grown older, through her symptoms, I have been able to recognize the changes my mother's brain has undergone over the years. One significant change is the overall reduction in brain volume. However, it seems that the areas most vital for cognitive abilities, such as the frontal lobe and hippocampus, are the ones that shrink the most. These areas are located behind our foreheads and play a vital role in our thinking processes, emotions, and who we are as individuals. The hippocampus, in particular, nestled deep within the temporal lobe, is essential for learning and memory. It saddens me to acknowledge that the hippocampus is susceptible to various neurological and psychiatric conditions as we witness its impact on my mother's illness.

Cortical Density
This term relates to the thinning of the brain's outer ridged surface due to a decrease in synaptic connections. The cerebral cortex, home to neuronal cell bodies and the brain's outer wrinkled layer, also becomes thinner as we age. The thinning follows a pattern similar to volume loss and is especially prominent in the frontal lobes and certain areas of the temporal lobe. Reduced density results in fewer connections, potentially slowing cognitive processing (Columbia University, 2021).

White Matter
Composed of myelinated nerve fibers bundled into tracts, white matter transmits nerve signals between brain cells. It's believed that myelin diminishes with age, slowing processing and undermining cognitive function. The white matter is a comprehensive system of neural connections integrating all four brain lobes and the limbic system, the brain's emotional hub (Columbia University, 2021).

Neurotransmitter Systems
As I watched my parents age, I had no idea their brains could start to produce different chemical levels affecting their neurotransmitters and protein

production, consequently leading to cognitive function decline. In light of these changes, aging adults might encounter challenges such as difficulty remembering names or words, decreased attention span, or a reduced ability to multitask (Columbia University, 2021).

In the aging brain, neuron death begins, and cells start producing a compound known as beta-amyloid. Typically associated with Alzheimer's disease, beta-amyloid can also be found in the brains of those simply aging. The presence of beta-amyloid plaques in the brain could indicate Alzheimer's disease, while the absence of prions in these plaques might suggest normal aging (Columbia University, 2021). What all this means is that it becomes increasingly challenging for older individuals to independently take care of themselves as their brains age.

Dementia

Dementia is an overarching term that describes a group of symptoms associated with a decline in memory, reasoning, or other thinking skills. It's not a specific disease, but several different diseases may cause dementia. Among the various types of dementia, Alzheimer's disease is the most common, accounting for an estimated 60 to 80 percent of cases (Mayo Clinic, 2021).

Vascular dementia, which often occurs after a stroke, is the second most common dementia type. Other types include dementia with Lewy bodies (DLB), frontotemporal dementia, mixed dementia, Parkinson's disease dementia, and others such as Huntington's disease and Creutzfeldt-Jakob disease (Mayo Clinic, 2021).

The signs and symptoms of dementia can vary greatly, but typically at least two of the following core mental functions must be significantly impaired to be considered dementia: memory, communication and language, ability to focus and pay attention, reasoning and judgment, and visual perception (Alzheimer's Society, n.d). I witnessed all of these with both of my parents. People with dementia often experience problems with short-term memory, such as keeping track of a purse or wallet, paying bills, planning and preparing meals, remembering appointments, or traveling out of the neighborhood. Over time, the symptoms of dementia tend to worsen (Alzheimer's Society, n.d). One of the first signs I noticed with my father was him simply forgetting if he ate or not. I would stock the fridge and freezer, only to return to little being consumed.

Besides memory loss, other early symptoms of dementia can include difficulty completing familiar tasks, confusion with time or place, trouble understanding visual images and spatial relationships, new problems with words in speaking or writing, and decreased or poor judgment. Personality changes, apathy, and withdrawal from social activities are also common. My father was the king of bad decision-making and poor judgment in the beginning. It would be only thirty days after I noticed his failing mental health that I would check his financial situation and be shocked at some frivolous and ridiculous purchases he had made. A canoe, for instance, despite him being afraid of open water. Six sets of professional chef's knives, despite his loathing cooking.

As dementia progresses, more severe symptoms appear, including physical and mobility changes, difficulty swallowing, and significant memory loss. It's important to remember that dementia is not a normal part of aging, and if any of these signs or symptoms are noticed, it is important to seek medical attention for a proper diagnosis and treatment plan.

Memory Loss

As a woman whose mother has Alzheimer's and dementia and having lost my father to dementia, I understand that memory loss is a common aspect of the aging process. It's something I have personally observed in my parents. There are various signs and symptoms that indicate memory loss in older adults, and they can range from mild forgetfulness to more severe indicators.

For instance, my mother would often misplace everyday items like her glasses or keys, and she would frequently ask the same questions repeatedly. I began to notice that she sometimes got lost in familiar places, like the same grocery store she visited for years. Simple tasks that she used to handle with ease, like balancing a checkbook or following a recipe, would be impossible for her now. You may also observe a decline in the ability to concentrate and focus, and my mom would sometimes struggle with abstract thinking. She also stopped reading books. Initially, I thought it was because her eyesight was fading, but in hindsight (pun intended), I realize her cognitive decline was to blame.

I want to emphasize that not all memory loss in aging parents is a cause for alarm regarding serious cognitive declines, such as Alzheimer's disease or other forms of dementia. Normal age-related memory loss usually doesn't significantly impact daily functioning, unlike pathological memory loss. However, if memory changes start interfering with your parent's daily life or are accompanied by other cognitive problems, it could indicate a more serious issue.

In my mother's case, I noticed disorientation and confusion even in familiar settings, and she began to find it difficult to complete simple daily tasks like brushing her teeth. She experienced language problems, such as forgetting words or using inappropriate substitutes. Moreover, her mood and behavior changed so much. She went from a loving mom to an unpredictable, angry person. Whenever memory problems persist, worsen over time, or severely affect daily life, it's important to consult a healthcare provider for evaluation. This is essential to rule out underlying conditions or illnesses that may be contributing to these issues.

For example, one medical condition that surfaced for both my parents on more than one occasion is a urinary tract infection (UTI). During my mother's first psychotic episode, which we thought to be a result of her dementia, was that it was not. I learned that it is quite common for aging people to develop UTIs. The symptoms in seniors are different from those of a younger person. The doctor explained that because my mother didn't know she had the bacterial infection, it worsened and led her to psychosis.

At the time, this was not something I would have ever considered. The UTI that she had caused her to hallucinate and become extremely paranoid and violent. She began calling on her condo board and building manager, yelling and screaming that someone was breaking into her locker in the garage. She was absolutely out of her mind. She covered all the mirrors in her home because she thought "they" were coming for her. She called my brothers and me incessantly about all the "crazy" people around her and her building. It was only when we were able to get her to the emergency room that we learned this was a physical infection, and with a strong course of antibiotics, her acute psychosis tapered off. She returned home but should have been moved to a memory care facility at that time because she was still a threat to her own well-being; she was still demented.

What Is Normal Aging?

Aging is a natural part of life that everyone goes through, but the way individuals age can vary widely. Aging affects everyone differently, depending on genetics, lifestyle choices, and environmental factors.

Normal Aging

As we age, our bodies naturally go through certain changes. I have included examples of normal aging:

- **Slower metabolism and weight gain**: With age, our metabolism slows down, and we may gain weight more easily.
- **Skin changes**: Skin becomes thinner, less elastic, and more fragile as we age. Wrinkles, age spots, and dryness are also common.
- **Bone, joint, and muscle changes**: Bones tend to shrink in size and density, which can

weaken them and make them more susceptible to fracture. Muscles lose strength and flexibility, and joints may become stiff and lose their range of motion.
- **Cardiovascular changes**: Over time, the heart and blood vessels naturally stiffen, leading to conditions like hypertension (high blood pressure).
- **Sensory changes**: Vision and hearing may decline, and changes in taste, smell, and touch are also common.
- **Cognitive changes**: It's normal for certain cognitive functions to decline with age, such as the speed of information processing and certain aspects of memory.

Abnormal Aging

While some decline in physical and cognitive function is expected with age, certain symptoms or conditions can be signs of abnormal or irregular aging. Below are some examples:

- **Severe memory loss or dementia**: While mild forgetfulness can be a part of normal aging, severe memory loss, confusion, personality changes, or other dramatic shifts in cognitive abilities may be signs of a serious condition like Alzheimer's disease or another type of dementia.
- **Major changes in mobility or balance**: Difficulty walking, frequent falls, or major

changes in balance or mobility can be signs of abnormal aging.

- **Rapid, unexplained weight loss or gain**: Significant weight loss or gain without a clear reason could be a sign of a serious health problem.
- **Persistent fatigue or depression**: While everyone feels tired or down from time to time, chronic fatigue or depression isn't a normal part of aging and may be a sign of an underlying issue.
- **Unexplained or persistent pain**: Chronic pain is not a normal part of aging and should always be evaluated by a health care professional.
- **Sudden or severe changes in vision or hearing**: While gradual changes in vision or hearing are normal, sudden or severe changes are not and should be evaluated.

We all age differently, so what's normal for one person might not be for another. It's always important to consult with a healthcare professional about any concerns or changes in physical or mental health. Aging isn't a disease but a complex process that can be influenced by a variety of factors. Regular check-ups and preventive care can help to ensure that any potential issues are detected and addressed early.

Chronic Conditions and Daily Life

Chronic ailments can significantly affect aging parents in several ways, and three significant impacts involve physical limitations, mental health implications, and potential financial burdens.

We need to be mindful that chronic diseases often lead to physical limitations that restrict our parent's daily activities and independence. Conditions such as arthritis can make simple tasks like opening jars or walking stairs challenging, while ailments like heart disease or COPD (Chronic Obstructive Pulmonary Disease) can lead to reduced stamina and difficulty in breathing, thus limiting physical exertion. For example, my dad was once an avid gardener, but eventually, he found he was unable to continue this hobby due to joint pain and fatigue.

We can't ignore the mental health implications of chronic diseases. With the onset of chronic ailments, our aging parents may face a diminished quality of life, leading to feelings of depression, anxiety, and social isolation. For instance, if your parent suffers from Parkinson's disease, they might experience cognitive decline, resulting in reduced social interaction and increased feelings of isolation. Furthermore, the constant worry about their health status could trigger anxiety, making it harder for them to enjoy their later years.

The financial burden is a critical consequence of chronic ailments in our aging parents. The cost of long-term medical care, medication, and the potential need for assisted living or home care can add up, straining your family's financial resources. For example, an aging parent with a chronic condition like diabetes requires constant monitoring, medication, and regular check-ups, which, over time, can lead to substantial medical bills. This is especially significant in regions where healthcare is costly or for those without comprehensive medical insurance.

As we've traversed the complex landscapes of the aging brain, we've come to appreciate both its elegance and resilience. We've looked into the various changes that occur over time–from the unavoidable neuronal decline to the plasticity that allows the brain to continually learn and adapt, even as the years roll by. We've seen that while aging brings about certain transformations, it is not synonymous with inevitable decline. With the right interventions and understanding, we can support and promote cognitive health in the later stages of life.

The insights we've gleaned here provide a backdrop for the practical measures that can be taken to enhance the lives of our aging parents. It's not merely about understanding the changes but about translating that understanding into actions that can create a safe, nurturing environment for our loved ones.

I would like to move into the tangible, day-to-day implications of aging and what we can do to navigate them effectively. We will explore the realm of home safety and modifications, practical and essential strategies to help our aging parents maintain their independence, enjoy a high quality of life, and thrive in a comfortable, safe, and familiar environment. By understanding and accommodating the physical realities of aging, we can contribute significantly to the well-being of our parents.

Chapter 2

Home Safety and Modification

* * *

The secret to getting started is breaking your overwhelming tasks into small manageable tasks, and then starting on the first one.— Mark Twain

Peer Spotlight: Alex

First off, let me introduce myself. My name is Alex, and I met Elizabeth at a day program for dementia. When she mentioned that she was looking to write a book to help those stuck in the sandwich generation, I offered to contribute by writing up some of my experience with helping my parents. I've recently taken on the daunting yet rewarding task of making my parents' home more elderly-friendly. My parents, both in their late seventies, have expressed their wish to age in place, and I want to do everything possible to make that safe and comfortable for them.

As they've aged, mobility has become an issue for both of them. I noticed that their multi-story home was filled with steep stairs, loose rugs, and furniture that obstructed paths. Additionally, the bathrooms weren't equipped with safety features like grab bars and non-slip surfaces, which worried me, given the high incidence of falls in bathrooms among seniors.

My first step in this journey was to conduct a thorough walk-through of their home, making a list of potential hazards and areas that could be improved. During this walk-through, I noticed things like poor lighting, which could lead to trips and falls, and hard-to-reach shelves and cupboards in the kitchen, making daily tasks more dangerous for my parents.

I went ahead and hired a Certified Aging in Place Specialist (CAPS). They're a professional trained in the needs of the elderly, home modifications, and common remodeling projects (Hager, 2019). They were able to provide advice on how to prioritize my modifications, keeping both safety and my parents' personal comfort in mind.

The kitchen was our first target. We replaced the high cabinets with pull-down shelving units and installed a new stove with front controls to prevent overreaching. We also ensured that the floor was smooth, non-slip, and easy to clean, preventing any tripping or slipping hazards.

Next, we worked on the bathrooms, installing grab bars near the toilet and in the shower, and we even decided to convert the tub into a walk-in shower with a seat. We also added non-slip floor mats and ensured that the sink was wheelchair accessible, just in case that becomes a necessity in the future.

The lighting throughout the house needed improvement,

so we added automatic motion-sensor lights to ensure all areas were well-lit when in use.

We added a stair lift to the steep staircase, but I also helped them convert the downstairs study into a bedroom, minimizing the need to use stairs.

Another important modification we made was removing all the high-pile carpets and replacing them with low-pile ones to reduce tripping hazards. We also made sure to keep paths clear of furniture and other obstacles, especially in high-traffic areas.

It was important for my parents to maintain their independence, so we included smart home technologies to assist them. Voice-activated controls for lights, thermostats, and other devices, as well as a video doorbell, added an extra layer of convenience and security.

The whole process took a few months, and although it was an investment, it was worth it. Seeing my parents move more confidently and safely in their home brought a huge relief. I knew I couldn't eliminate all risks, but the modifications significantly reduced the chances of a major accident.

This journey of modifying my parents' home for their safe aging has been rewarding and enlightening. It's prompted conversations within our family about what aging with dignity should look like and has allowed me to give back to my parents in a meaningful way.

Assessing Your Home

If you are reaching the point of having your aging parents live with you, or you need to keep *their* home safe, assessing homes for safety risks is a vital step to ensure their well-being. As we age, the likelihood of accidents happening at home can increase due to changes in physical capabilities, sensory impairments, chronic illnesses, or cognitive changes.

What Is Home Assessment Safety?

A Home safety assessment is an evaluation of a person's living space to identify potential hazards that could lead to injury. This assessment is especially important for older adults, individuals with disabilities, or anyone who has a higher risk of falls or injuries. The aim is to modify or eliminate any risks and ensure the home is safe and comfortable (Baum, 2023). These assessments are important for a number of reasons:

1. Preventing accidents: A home safety assessment helps identify risks that could lead to falls, accidents, and other safety incidents. This is especially critical for older adults or people with mobility issues, where a fall could have serious health consequences.
2. Promoting independence: By ensuring the home environment is safe and accessible, home safety assessments can help individuals, particularly seniors or people with disabilities, live independently for longer.
3. Peace of mind: Knowing that potential hazards have been identified and addressed can provide peace of mind for the individual and their family.
4. Saving costs: Prevention is always better and more cost-effective than dealing with the consequences of an accident.

A variety of professionals can conduct home safety assessments, depending on the individual's specific needs and situation:

Occupational therapists (OTs): OTs are often involved in home safety assessments, particularly for individuals who have recently been discharged from the hospital, have chronic health conditions, or have mobility issues. OTs can provide recommendations for home modifications and adaptive equipment.

Physical therapists (PTs): Similar to OTs, PTs can assess the safety of the home environment, particularly as it relates to an individual's mobility and physical health.

Certified aging-in-place specialists (CAPS): CAPS professionals have specialized training in modifying homes for older adults to safely and comfortably age in place.

Home inspectors: For general home safety issues like electrical wiring, structural issues, and radon or mold detection, a certified home inspector might be called upon.

Fire department: Some local fire departments offer home safety checks, particularly related to fire safety.

Home health care providers: Nurses or aides are examples of home health care providers who can also conduct basic safety checks as part of their duties.

The scope of the assessment can vary but typically includes things like ensuring there's proper lighting, checking that rugs and cords aren't tripping hazards, making sure there are grab bars in the bathroom, assessing the need for stairlifts or ramps, checking the condition of stairs and handrails, verifying smoke and carbon monoxide detectors are present and functioning, and so on.

How to Assess Your Home

I know that prior to my own mother taking residence in a care home, I wanted to be sure my own home was a safe space for her to visit. I wanted to offer some general areas to look at when assessing the home for safety risks, specifically for aging adults:

Entryways and Exits: Look at all the places where someone can enter or leave the house. Are there any steps or stairs that could be difficult to navigate? Is there a sturdy handrail? Is there proper lighting to prevent trips and falls? Consider installing ramps for easier access if necessary.

Flooring: Loose rugs, cords, or clutter can be trip hazards. Make sure all pathways are clear and consider removing or securing rugs to the floor to prevent slipping. Ensure that the flooring is not slippery and is in good condition.

Stairs: If the house has multiple levels, stairs can be a major hazard. Handrails should be on both sides, and stairs should be well-lit. If mobility is a significant issue, it may be necessary to install a chair lift.

Bathroom: This is one of the most hazardous places due to the risk of slipping. Install grab bars near the toilet and in the shower or tub. A shower chair and handheld shower head can make bathing safer. Non-slip mats are also crucial.

Kitchen: Are the counters at a comfortable height? Are commonly used items easily accessible? If not, reorganize for accessibility and safety. Stovetop burners and appliances should have automatic shutoffs for safety.

Lighting: Proper lighting is essential, especially for individuals with declining vision. Make sure all areas of the house are well-lit. Nightlights in hallways, bathrooms, and bedrooms can be helpful.

Emergency Exits: Everyone in the house should be able to get out quickly in case of an emergency. Check all windows and doors to ensure they can be easily opened.

Medication Safety: Medications should be stored in a safe, easy-to-access location. Consider pill organizers to ensure the correct medication and dosage are taken at the right time.

Security: Install security systems or alarms, especially if your elderly parent has a cognitive disorder like dementia. Door alarms can alert you if they try to wander away from home.

Furniture: Make sure the furniture is sturdy and will not tip over easily. Corners and sharp edges should be covered to prevent injury.

Every individual's needs will differ depending on their health status, mobility, and cognitive abilities. You might want to consider working with an occupational therapist or a professional who specializes in eldercare home modifications to get a comprehensive understanding of the modifications required for your specific situation.

Home Modification Suggestions

Listen, when you are smack in the middle of caring for aging parents, you are swimming in uncertainty and beyond overwhelmed. You are dizzy with confusion, exhaustion, worry, and so much more. You run lists and appointments through your head, trying to keep your head above water. In order to reduce some of that potential worry, you can ensure the home of your parent(s), and yourself are safe.

Home Modification Tips:

- **Improving lighting:** Poorly lit areas can increase the risk of falls. Install bright lights in every room and hallway, and consider motion-sensor lights for ease of use. Don't forget to illuminate stairways and outdoor walkways as well.
- **Railing installation:** Install handrails on both sides of any stairs inside and outside the house. This provides additional support when going up and down the stairs.
- **Bathroom adjustments:** Install grab bars in the shower, by the toilet, and near the bathroom sink. Consider using a shower chair and a handheld showerhead. An elevated toilet seat can also make it easier to stand up and sit down.
- **Clear pathways:** Ensure all walkways are clear of clutter and obstacles. This can help prevent trips and falls.

- **Flooring changes:** Avoid rugs or secure them well to prevent slipping. Consider replacing slick flooring with a slip-resistant surface.
- **Kitchen adjustments:** Store commonly used items at waist level to avoid the need for stooping or reaching. Consider installing pull-out shelves or drawers for easier access.
- **Doorway modifications:** Widen doorways to accommodate a wheelchair or walker if necessary. Install lever-style doorknobs, which are easier to handle than round knobs.
- **Home entry:** If stairs at the home entrance pose a problem, consider installing a ramp.

Safety Checklist

- **Smoke and carbon monoxide detectors:** Make sure you install them on every level of the home and including any outside sleeping areas. Test them regularly to ensure they're working.
- **Emergency numbers:** Keep a list of emergency numbers in an easily accessible area. This should include numbers for doctors, the nearest hospital, and loved ones who can help in an emergency.
- **Avoid tripping hazards:** Remove or secure loose rugs, clear clutter, and tidy up loose cords. As we age, we tend to be less focused on where

we are walking, making tripping hazards a real concern.

- **Non-Slip mats:** Install non-slip mats in the bathroom, particularly in the bathtub and shower. Far too many seniors have avoidable falls in the bathroom, causing hip fractures and more. This simple addition can help.
- **Adequate lighting:** As previously mentioned, ensure all areas of the house are well-lit, particularly stairs and hallways. The installation of motion lights is a fantastic idea as our parents may forget to hit the light on their way to the bathroom.
- **Secure handrails and grab bars:** Inspect existing handrails and grab bars regularly to make sure they're secure. Over time, these can wear down or become loose, presenting an accident waiting to happen.
- **Safe storage of medications and cleaning supplies:** Keep all medications and cleaning supplies in a safe location. Make sure they're properly sealed, clearly labeled, and stored away from food.
- **Accessible emergency exits:** Make sure all potential exits are easily accessible in case of an emergency. For example, if there is a fire, you don't want clutter blocking the safest exit. All doors and windows should be free of obstacles.
- **Regular check-ups on heating and cooling systems:** Make sure heating and

cooling systems are working properly and maintained regularly. As our parents age, they can find operating these systems tricky. You now have the option of keeping their thermostat live on your phone, helping you monitor if the temperature becomes too high or low.

- **Fire extinguisher:** Keep a fire extinguisher in the kitchen and any other area that represents a significant fire risk. Make sure your aging parents know how to use it. If they struggle with a standard extinguisher, they do make smaller versions or a spray canister system.
- **Alert systems:** Whether our parents are living with us or independent, investing in alert systems brings peace of mind. My grandmother had one over twenty years ago, and with the advanced technology, they are easier than ever. There are multiple subscription services, so I do recommend you research the best option for your family. The benefit is always knowing if your parents need help. An alert will appear on your own phone, offering you the ability to speak into the room where your parent may be in distress. They are all camera compatible as well, so you can get a snapshot of what may be happening in their home in emergency situations.

By following these tips and consistently checking each point on the home safety checklist, you can help make your home a safer and more accessible place for your aging parents.

Interactive Element

When you enter the world of caring for your aging parents, you will find yourself suffocating with all you need to remember. I suggest that you create a checklist for health and safety. Each day, you can travel down the list, checking off what needs to be addressed.

I am going to offer an example of a checklist for you to follow. Feel free to adapt this list or create one of your own to include specific items your parents need.

Home Safety

- **Staircases:** Install handrails on both sides of staircases. Ensure stairs are well-lit and free of clutter.
- **Bathrooms:** Install grab bars in the shower, by the toilet, and by the bathtub. Consider non-slip mats or stickers for the shower and bathtub.
- **Flooring:** Remove any throw rugs or secure them with non-slip pads. Check for any uneven flooring or cords that can cause tripping.
- **Lighting:** Ensure all rooms, hallways, and stairs are well-lit. Consider night lights for nighttime navigation.

- **Kitchen:** Keep commonly used items within easy reach. Make sure all appliances are functioning properly and are easy to use.

Health Safety

- **Medications:** Keep a current list of medications, doses, and schedules. Consider a pill organizer.
- **Doctor appointments**: Maintain a calendar of all medical appointments.
- **Nutrition:** Ensure a healthy diet is being followed. Consider meal prep or delivery services if cooking is a concern.
- **Exercise:** Encourage regular physical activity, as approved by their doctor.
- **Mental health**: Monitor for signs of loneliness, depression, or anxiety. Provide social interaction.

Emergency Preparedness

- **Emergency contacts:** Have a list of all important phone numbers in an easily accessible location.
- **Emergency plan:** Create a plan in case of a fire, natural disaster, or medical emergency.
- **Check-in system:** Consider daily check-in calls or visits.

- **Medical alert system:** Consider a medical alert device that can be worn and used to call for help.
- **First aid kit:** Have a well-stocked first aid kit and ensure caregivers know how to use it.

General Caregiving

- **Caregiver support:** Make sure caregivers have a support network and are taking care of their own health.
- **Respite care:** Plan for backup or respite care when primary caregivers need a break.
- **Financial matters:** Ensure all bills, insurance, and financial matters are in order.
- **Legal matters:** Consider a consultation with an elder law attorney to ensure all legal matters are in order, such as power of attorney, living wills, etc.

Now let's turn our attention to the next important aspect of caring for aging parents: navigating the complex terrain of legal and financial matters. In the upcoming chapter, we will travel into the essential considerations and steps required to ensure our parents' financial stability, protect their assets, and address any legal concerns that may arise. By proactively addressing these matters, we can further enhance the support and care we provide, enabling our aging parents to enjoy a fulfilling life and offer less worry for all involved.

Chapter 3

Navigating Legal and Financial Matters

** * ***

To care for those who once cared for us is one of the highest honors.—Tia Walker

Peer Spotlight: Susan

I'm finding that life really has a way of making a full circle, doesn't it? I mean, here I am, sandwiched in the middle of raising my children while also caring for my parents, who have given me so much. When Elizabeth asked me to contribute to her book, I thought I could share the part of my journey that shines a light on legal and financial matters.

I've learned it's essential to have a solid plan in place to protect my parents and their wishes as they age. Legal documents and estate planning might not be the most fun topic at *the Sunday dinner table, but it's a conversation we absolutely must have.*

We started looking at a will. It's important to clarify how my parents want their assets to be distributed after their passing. They have spent a lifetime working hard for what they have, and their wishes should be honored in how their possessions and financial assets are allocated.

We also considered a living will. It's a bit scary to think about, but it outlines the medical care my parents would want if they were too ill or incapacitated to express those decisions themselves. I want to ensure that their wishes are respected and carried out exactly as they would want.

We then talked about durable power of attorney for healthcare and finances. These are separate documents, but both are incredibly important. This way, my siblings and I can make informed decisions about their healthcare and manage their financial affairs if they're unable to do so.

One complex topic we tackled was trusts. They can be a bit intricate, but they're a fantastic way to manage their estate, especially when it comes to reducing estate taxes and bypassing the often lengthy probate process.

We made sure to keep beneficiary designations on financial products like life insurance and retirement accounts up-to-date, too. That way, these funds will go directly to the beneficiaries named without having to go through probate.

Next up was a letter of intent. This document isn't legally binding, but it does serve as a guiding document for my siblings and me, providing insight into any specific requests or wishes that my parents may have for when they're gone.

Navigating the golden years with my parents is a journey

filled with respect, sleepless nights, love, and, sometimes, difficult conversations. But preparing for these eventualities is a way to honor their lives and ensure their wishes are fulfilled. It's important to work with a qualified attorney to navigate all these complex legalities, but it brings peace of mind knowing that when the time comes, I can focus on cherishing their memories and not grappling with legal complications.

A Guide to Estate Planning

Embarking on the journey of estate planning can feel like a monumental task. But by breaking it down into manageable steps and seeking help when needed, it doesn't have to be so intimidating. As a woman who has juggled the care of both parents, I'd like to share the practical guide I've put together to navigate through estate planning for the elderly:

1. **Start the conversation:** Initiate an open and honest conversation with your elderly parents about their estate planning. Discuss their wishes, concerns, and any specific instructions they have regarding their assets and medical care.
2. **Gather information:** Create a comprehensive inventory of your parent's assets, including real estate, bank accounts, investments, retirement accounts, insurance policies, and valuable personal belongings. Make a list of their debts and obligations as well.
3. **Estate planning documents:** Encourage your parents to create or update essential estate

planning documents, such as a will, living will (advance healthcare directive), durable power of attorney, and healthcare proxy. These documents will ensure their wishes are legally protected and followed in the event of incapacity or death.

4. **Choose an executor and healthcare proxy:** Help your parents select a trustworthy and reliable executor who will be responsible for managing their estate after their passing. Additionally, assist them in designating a healthcare proxy who can make medical decisions on their behalf if they become unable to do so.

5. **Beneficiary designations:** Review the beneficiary designations on their financial accounts, retirement plans, and life insurance policies. Ensure the named beneficiaries are up to date and align with your parent's wishes.

6. **Long-term care planning:** Discuss potential long-term care needs and options with your parents. Explore long-term care insurance, Medicaid eligibility, and available community resources. If necessary, consult with an elder law attorney to understand the financial implications and plan for long-term care costs.

7. **Tax planning:** Consult with a qualified tax professional to understand the potential tax implications of your parent's estate plan. They

can provide guidance on minimizing estate taxes and maximizing available exemptions.

8. **Organize important documents:** Help your parents gather and organize their important documents in a secure location. This includes birth certificates, marriage certificates, social security cards, property deeds, financial statements, insurance policies, and estate planning documents. Keep copies of these documents in a safe place and inform your parents' trusted individuals of their whereabouts.

9. **Review and update regularly:** Estate plans should be reviewed periodically to ensure they remain current and reflect any changes in your parents' wishes or circumstances. Encourage your parents to revisit their plan every few years or after significant life events, such as the birth of grandchildren or the death of a loved one.

10. **Seek professional guidance:** Estate planning can be complex, and it's advisable to seek assistance from professionals such as estate planning attorneys, financial advisors, and tax experts. They can provide personalized guidance and ensure that your parent's estate plan is legally sound and aligned with their goals.

Managing Aging Parents' Finances and Retirement Planning

When I was swimming in the responsibilities of taking care of both parents, the task of assuming control over their finances became increasingly complex and sensitive. It's important to approach this responsibility with the utmost care, respect, and transparency. Allow me to share some valuable tips on effectively managing your parent(s) finances.

Open Communication: Establish open and honest communication with your parent(s) about their financial situation as early as possible. Discuss their wishes and concerns regarding their finances and ensure they understand the need for your involvement in the future. For instance, sit down with your parent(s) and have a candid conversation about their financial status, including their income, expenses, assets, and any existing debts or obligations.

Legal Documentation: Ensure that they have the necessary legal documents in place, such as a durable power of attorney and a healthcare proxy. These documents grant you the legal authority to manage your parents' finances and make decisions on their behalf when they are no longer able to do so. For example, help your parents consult with an attorney to create or update their legal documents, ensuring that they accurately reflect their current wishes and appoint you as their designated representative.

Financial Inventory: Create a comprehensive inventory of your parent's financial accounts, assets, liabilities, and other important documents. This includes bank accounts, investment portfolios, insurance policies, real estate holdings, and any outstanding loans or debts. For instance, compile a spreadsheet or use financial management software to organize and track all the relevant financial information, making it easily accessible when needed.

Budgeting and Bill Payments: Work with your parent(s) to establish a budget that aligns with their income, expenses, and future needs. Set up a system for managing bill payments, such as automatic payments or online banking, to ensure their financial obligations are met on time. Review your parent's recurring expenses, such as utility bills, mortgage or rent payments, insurance premiums, and healthcare costs, and help them set up reminders or automated payments to simplify the process.

Financial Monitoring: Regularly monitor their financial accounts and transactions to detect any suspicious activity or signs of financial exploitation. Stay alert for unusual withdrawals, unfamiliar charges, or sudden changes in spending patterns.

Use online banking platforms or financial management tools to monitor account activity and set up alerts for unusual transactions. Review bank statements and credit card bills on a monthly basis.

Seek Professional Assistance: Consider engaging the services of a financial planner, notary, accountant, or elder law attorney who specializes in senior financial matters. They can provide expert advice, help you navigate complex financial situations, and ensure you comply with all legal and tax obligations. Consult with a financial planner to create a long-term financial plan for them, taking into account their retirement goals, healthcare expenses, and potential long-term care needs.

Regular Review and Communication: Schedule regular meetings with your parents to review their financial status, address any concerns, and make necessary adjustments. Keep them informed about their financial affairs, involving them in decision-making as much as possible. Plan quarterly or semi-annual meetings to discuss financial matters with them, allowing them to have a say in their financial decisions and keeping them engaged in the process.

Managing your parents' finances is a significant responsibility, and it's important to act in their best interests while respecting their autonomy. Be patient, compassionate, and involve them as much as possible in the decision-making process to maintain their dignity and sense of control.

Understanding Insurance Options

While caring for my aging parents, I've come to realize the importance of exploring various avenues when it comes to their health insurance and long-term care options. I understand firsthand the challenges faced by individuals with limited income, as navigating the intricate world of healthcare can be a web of confusion and anxiety. To alleviate some of this burden, I've taken the initiative to break down the necessary steps and available options, making the process more manageable and easier to understand.

Medicaid: The first option to consider is Medicaid. This is a federal and state program that helps with medical costs for some people with limited income and resources. Medicaid programs must cover certain populations and health services, such as elderly people, people with disabilities, and some low-income adults and children.

Eligibility varies state by state, as each has its own criteria. In many states, more people can qualify under expanded Medicaid programs. It's important to check the state's policy and income bracket to determine eligibility.

Medicare: Medicare is the federal health insurance

program for people who are 65 or older. It consists of several parts (Trovato, 2023):

- Part A covers hospital stays, care in a skilled nursing facility, hospice care, and some home health care. Most people don't pay a premium for Part A because they or a spouse already paid for it through their payroll taxes while working.
- Part B covers certain doctor's services, outpatient care, medical supplies, and preventive services. A premium is usually required for Part B.
- Part D adds prescription drug coverage. This, too, usually requires a premium.
- Medicare Advantage (Part C), an alternative to traditional Medicare, combines Part A, Part B, and usually Part D. It's offered by private companies approved by Medicare.

Long-term Care Insurance: Long-term care insurance is a policy designed to cover at least some of your costs if you have a chronic medical condition, a disability, or a disorder such as Alzheimer's disease. Most policies will reimburse you for care given in a variety of places, like your home, a nursing home, or an assisted living facility. However, they can be expensive, and premiums may increase over time. So, it's essential to consider this financial commitment.

Another reason we need to be diligent about this insurance is to protect our parents from themselves. Allow me to explain. My mother was attempting to protect herself and us in case of any medical issue. In fact, when she was about 60, she took out a long-term insurance policy.

When she moved out from living independently, about 15 years after she had taken the policy on, and I cleaned out her condo to sell, I went through her filing cabinet, which in her mind was very organized, I found said insurance policy and called the insurance company to activate her coverage. When I called, they said she had canceled the policy!

After some investigating, we learned that she canceled it the same day as her diagnosis. She canceled it out of anger. She did everything right to cover herself if she needed long-term care (SPECIFIC to memory care). She never told any of us, her children, about this policy. And then her disease made her cancel it!

We even managed to reinstate it because we were able to prove from the doctor's notes that the timeline was aligned with her rickety signature of the request to cancel. The lesson here is you may have to search your parent's home for these types of situations. It is vital to pay attention to everything when doing so.

PACE: Programs of All-Inclusive Care for the Elderly (PACE) is a Medicare and Medicaid program that helps people meet their healthcare needs in the community instead of going to a nursing home or other care facility. PACE covers medical, social service, and long-term care costs for frail people. It may be an option for them if they are eligible for nursing home care, can live safely in the community at the time of enrollment, and live in a PACE service area.

Veterans Health Administration: If either of your parents served in the military, they might be eligible for veterans' benefits from the Department of Veterans Affairs (VA). The VA provides a standard healthcare package that includes preventative, primary, and specialty care, as well as prescription drugs. The VA also offers long-term care services.

Planning and Choosing Insurance and Long-Term Care

Assessing the Needs: Understanding the type and amount of care your parents might need is the first step. Do they require help with daily activities? Are they dealing with a chronic condition? Are there memory issues to consider? These factors will dictate the type of coverage we should seek.

Research: I suggest comparing the different insurance options available. This involves understanding what each policy covers, the costs involved, the network of healthcare providers, and the limitations of each policy.

Financial Planning: In my father's case, I had to dig into his income and savings because I had to figure out what he was able to afford. He was way less financially secure than my mother. It may be advisable to discuss these issues with a financial advisor.

Consult a Professional: Navigating insurance policies can be complex. Therefore, I suggest the assistance of a geriatric care insurance specialist. Anytime I had the ability to speak to a professional about the steps involved in my parents' care, I jumped at it.

Interactive Element

Here are 7 helpful steps to walk through when creating a budget plan for elder care.

1. Understand Their Financial Situation: The first step to budgeting for elderly care is to understand the full financial picture. This might require some delicate conversations, as some parents may not be comfortable sharing their financial information. Start by gathering information on their income, savings, and investments. Also, it's essential to understand their insurance coverage, especially health, and long-term care insurance, and any government assistance they might be eligible for, such as Medicare or Medicaid.

2. Identify Their Needs and Preferences: Evaluate the health and lifestyle needs of your parents. Do they require regular medical attention or assistance with daily activities? Would they prefer to stay at home or live in a care facility? Their needs and preferences will significantly impact your budget.

3. Calculate Costs: Once you understand their needs, begin researching the costs involved. Some potential expenses to consider include:

- in-home care services
- assisted living or nursing home costs
- medical expenses not covered by insurance
- medication costs
- mobility aids
- home modifications for safety and accessibility
- Also, don't forget about their ongoing living expenses, like utilities, groceries, transportation, and entertainment.

4. Create the Budget: Now, it's time to bring everything together and make the budget. List out all sources of income and all projected expenses. Remember, it's important to account for potential increases in costs over time due to inflation or increasing care needs.

5. Set Up an Emergency Fund: It's important to have some financial cushion for unforeseen expenses. If possible, establish an emergency fund that can cover at least 3 to 6 months of expenses. This would be important in situations like entering a long-term home, purchasing mobility equipment, or the passing of one parent.

6. Regularly Review and Adjust the Budget: Elderly care needs and costs can change over time, so it's vital to review and adjust your budget periodically. Keep an eye on any changes in your parents' health or lifestyle needs that might require budget adjustments.

7. Seek Professional Help if Necessary: If managing this budget becomes overwhelming or if your parents' situation is complex, consider seeking advice from a financial planner or elder care attorney. You have enough on your plate, so delegating some of these responsibilities would be helpful.

As I reflect on the wild journey of navigating legal and financial matters while caring for my parents, I am reminded of the immense responsibility that falls upon our shoulders. Through tireless efforts and countless hours of research, I have come to realize the profound impact that proper planning and informed decision-making can have on our loved one's well-being.

I quickly learned the invaluable lesson of the importance of being proactive, seeking professional guidance, and facing the daunting task of unraveling complex legal and financial webs head-on. As I turn the page and dive into the next chapter of communicating with family while caring for my remaining parent, I carry with me the resilience and determination that has brought me this far, knowing that open and honest dialogue will serve as the compass guiding my brothers and me through the challenges that lie ahead.

Chapter 4

Communicating With Siblings and Family Members

* * *

The greatest thing in family life is to take a hint when a hint is intended—and not to take a hint when a hint is not intended.
—Robert Frost

Peer Spotlight: Christine

Christine, a former colleague with whom I have remained in touch for the last number of years, offered to write her own account for this chapter. Christine and I have a lot in common as we both have been handling such similar situations with our mothers as their mental health declined. As my mother started to show signs of dementia around the same time as Christine's, we always used to find ourselves in the staff room bitching about our aging moms to each other. We learned together what the onset of dementia looked like. Back then, neither of us knew what was coming our way. Anyway, I will stop rambling and let her tell her story in her own words.

For most of my life, it was just me and my mom. She gave birth to my brother at age 16 and me at 18, and as she puts it, "We grew up together." Where was my brother, you ask? She gave full custody of him to our biological father. As hard as I try, I cannot think of a time when I wasn't traveling, going to concerts, or having spa days, all with my mom. We were best friends, and I miss her.

She is not dead. She is very much alive; she just isn't my mom. She is now a completely different human and one that I can barely tolerate. How did we get here? What went so wrong?

It was so gradual I missed it—every sign, every episode, I missed them all. I will hold on to that guilt for the rest of my life. She needed me, and I wasn't there.

Let's back up just a bit. Looking back now, I know exactly the first time my radar should have been more alert. It was five years ago, and I took my mom to bingo. She loved this game, the anticipation, the socialization, all of it. She had a favorite table and knew many of the regulars well. They would bake goods for each other and chat about their day.

So, there we were at bingo. I noticed her rummaging through her purse, and when I asked what she was looking for, she got angry. "I don't need you babysitting me; I am just getting my glasses out," she barked. Taken aback, I gently told her they were on the table in front of her. Halfway through the session, I asked her if she would like something to drink. After telling me she would like some water, I went to the concession stand to get just that. She took a few sips and immediately had a frown on her face. When I asked her what the issue was, she threw the water in my face.

Shocked and teary-eyed, I headed to the bathroom to clean up. Hair wet and make-up running, I returned to the table where my mother sat as if nothing had happened. When we got in the car to leave, I asked her why she had done that. "Are you stupid? I don't like that kind of water, and you should know that," she snarled.

Over the next five years, I would be spit at, slapped, yelled at, and have a lot of food thrown in my direction. She was angry and hostile and repeatedly told me to leave her alone, she had given her whole life to me, and now she wanted me to leave. I reached out to my estranged brother for reinforcements.

Together, we had to learn how to communicate with each other and our mother. We had never lived together and were virtual strangers. We had to listen to advice from doctors, therapists, and specialists and decipher what was best. We learned to give her space in the difficult moments. I had never dealt with anything remotely close to this before, so an issue with her brain never occurred to me. Until I received a call from a bus driver who had my mother on his bus screaming she was being kidnapped. Another passenger asked her if she had any children, and she yelled my name. They tracked me down, and I rushed to the bus. When I walked on, she crumpled in her seat and sobbed. We saw the doctor within an hour.

A day that started out with plans to meet up with friends ended with us, as a family, sitting in a doctor's *office and being told my mother had dementia. She was 69 years old at that time. Tests, scans, blood panels, all to tell me that my mother was gone. She had been gone.*

I immediately told the doctor I would have her live with me, and with one look from him, I knew we were past that point. I had confided in him all the episodes I could remember, and he felt for her safety, she needed to be in a care home.

Three years later and my mother only recalls her cat. I shit you not. She asks about this cat (who has since passed) every single day I visit. She believes I am the "hired help." Losing your mother in this way is beyond comprehension unless you have lived it. I mourn and grieve on an ongoing basis. I mourn the life and relationship we once had. I mourn her not having the ability to be a grandmother. This is not just unfair; it is cruel.

I don't know how much time I have left with her here on earth. I would be lying if I hadn't wished her suffering would end. I know my mother, and she would not want to live out her days this way. So, we wait. I visit, and I endure the ridicule and hostility in the hopes she may remember. It is exhausting and draining, but I will forever love her and the life we once shared.

Communicating With Elderly Parents

As I find myself in the role of a caregiver for my aging mother, I recognize the diverse dynamics that shape our relationships with our parents. Each of us has our own unique bond, whether it be a close connection or a more distant one. However, as the years pass by, we inevitably come face-to-face with the reality of our parents' aging, and the realization dawns that they now depend on our assistance. In this critical juncture, learning how to effectively communicate with them becomes paramount. Their health issues, such as memory loss or heart disease, add further complexity to the equation. They may harbor fears and anxieties about an uncertain future, yet it is essential to approach them with respect, avoiding any condescension or treating them like children. Although the roles may have reversed, I am mindful that I am not assuming a parental role; it is important to maintain that distinction. Communication, at its core, is built on understanding, empathy, and fostering meaningful connections. These elements take on even greater significance when interacting with aging parents, particularly those contending with medical conditions.

Importance of Communication With Aging Parents

As I witnessed my parents aging, I recognized the need to engage parents in challenging discussions that lie ahead. These conversations need to encompass various topics, including finances, medical requirements, the creation of wills, and more. To ensure a seamless process, it is important for us to comprehend the significance of effective communication with our parents.

Understanding Their Needs
As our parents age, their needs and capabilities change. We need to be aware of these changes and

provide the support they require. It's important to communicate effectively to understand their evolving needs and find the best ways to assist them. For instance, if you notice your parents forgetting routine tasks, they may benefit from assistance in organizing their day or managing their medications.

Preserving Dignity and Independence

One of the biggest fears many elderly people have is losing their independence. By communicating openly and honestly, we can understand how to support them in ways that respect their autonomy and dignity. For example, rather than assuming they can't handle a task and take it over, it would be better to ask and offer assistance.

Expressing Love and Care

Emotional well-being is just as important as physical health. By maintaining open lines of communication, we can express our love, concern, and care for our aging parents. This can reassure them that they are not alone and that they have a support system.

Addressing Medical Concerns

As people age, they are more likely to encounter various health issues. Regular communication allows you to stay updated on their health status, ensuring that any changes or concerns can be addressed promptly.

How to Communicate Effectively with Aging Parents

Now we know why it is important to communicate, but how do we accomplish this? Let's review some suggestions for taking that step.

Be Patient and Understanding
Aging can lead to slower cognitive processes and difficulties in expressing thoughts. It's important to be patient, listen carefully, and avoid interrupting or finishing sentences for them. And, as tempting and natural as it may seem, don't "quiz" your aging parents to see if their mental decline has gotten worse. We are not experts and it can be an upsetting approach for both parties—your parent and you, the caregiver.

Adapt Your Communication Style
Aging can bring about changes in hearing, vision, and cognitive ability, so you may need to speak more slowly, articulate more clearly, or use more straightforward language. If a parent has a medical condition like Alzheimer's, maintaining a calm, gentle tone and using simple, clear sentences can be beneficial.

Ask Open-Ended Questions
Instead of asking yes or no questions, use open-ended ones to promote conversation and gather more

information. For example, instead of asking, "Did you have lunch?" you might ask, "What did you have for lunch today?"

Involve Them in Decisions
As mentioned, there will be tough decisions heading your way regarding your parents. Whenever possible, involve them in decision-making processes, especially regarding their care. This respect for their autonomy can provide them with a sense of control and dignity.

Use Nonverbal Communication
If you have a parent suffering from a medical issue that affects their speech, words may become difficult. It is suggested to adopt other forms of communication that can convey love and support. Try a gentle touch, making eye contact, and spending time together because these can be just as meaningful as words.

Acknowledge Their Feelings
If they're feeling scared, frustrated, or depressed, it's important to validate those feelings. Empathizing with their situation can help them feel understood and supported.

For instance: If they are suffering from chronic pain, it's important to talk about how this affects them, not just physically but also emotionally. Saying something like, "I can see that you're in a lot of pain, and it's making life hard for you. How can I support you?" is a more empathetic approach than simply focusing on medical treatments.

Effective communication doesn't just mean talking; it also involves active listening. By listening empathetically, we can better understand our parents' needs, fears, and wishes, allowing us to provide them with the support they need as they navigate the challenges of aging.

Communication Strategies Between Family Members

Communicating and sharing caregiving responsibilities within the family is a complex endeavor that requires a boatload of patience, understanding, and compromise. In my own experience, as someone sandwiched between caring for my aging parents and my own family, it's clear that this is not a role for the faint-hearted. Let me help guide you through the process.

> **Open Communication:** It's essential to maintain open lines of communication. It's important to have frank discussions about each person's capacity and willingness to contribute and make sure everyone understands what is required in terms of time, effort, and money.
>
> Take my family, for example, when my mother's condition worsened, my brothers and I had a sit-

down discussion about how we could jointly support her. It was tough; many tears were shed, and some truths came out, but in the end, we developed a stronger understanding of each other's perspectives and abilities.

It is completely normal and expected to feel you cannot handle certain areas of your parent's care. You are not expected to do it all, and you will burn out if you try. Lean into your voice and be sure it is heard. Each family member should be brutally honest when it comes to assigning tasks. It is also vital to keep everyone in the loop.

Clearly Defining Roles: Having clearly defined roles and responsibilities doesn't mean that every little task needs to be assigned, but rather that overall areas of responsibility should be clear. One person could handle financial matters, while another might handle medical appointments, and so on. Divide and conquer is the best way to tackle these situations.

For instance, my brother naturally took up the role of managing our parents' healthcare, medications, and doctor appointments. I, being more comfortable with finances, took responsibility for their financial affairs and insurance matters. Just remember you will need to have the necessary permission in place to take over these matters (i.e., power of attorney).

Delegating Tasks: Delegation is an art that requires trust, respect, and clear communication. It's about acknowledging that you cannot do everything yourself and allowing others to share in the care. Be mindful of each family member's strengths, limitations, and availability when assigning tasks.

In my case, I had to delegate some tasks to my teenage children. At first, I was apprehensive about asking them to help with chores or with their grandparents, but it was a chance for them to step up and mature. They began helping with tasks such as grocery shopping, cooking meals, and spending time with their grandparents, and it was actually an enriching experience for everyone involved.

Balancing the Load: Remember that the division of tasks should be balanced, not necessarily equal. Factors such as proximity, available time, and other personal responsibilities should be considered. This approach ensures that no single person gets overwhelmed and everyone can contribute according to their abilities.

Regular Check-Ins: You should be planning regular check-ins to review the care plan and make necessary adjustments. These meetings can provide a space to air grievances, discuss challenges, and reassess how caregiving duties are divided.

In our family, we have monthly meetings when we discuss any concerns, changes in our parents' condition, and if anyone is feeling overburdened. Sometimes these discussions lead to redistributing tasks or bringing in outside help, such as a part-time caregiver.

Being part of the sandwich generation, caring for both parents and children is a delicate balance. But through open communication, clear roles, effective delegation, balanced responsibilities, and regular check-ins, you can ensure everyone in the family pulls their weight, strengthening your bond during a challenging time.

Dealing With Conflicts and Difficult Family Dynamics

Now, that all sounds feasible, right? But what if you come from a family who has never been close? What if you are estranged from your siblings? What if you dislike your parents and don't feel obligated to help? There are many variations to the family unit, and this will all play into this journey you are on.

I can feel the weight of your concern. It's not an easy topic we're about to discuss, but I wanted to explore some common situations we might encounter and how we can navigate them.

1. Unequal Burden of Care: It's quite common to have one sibling shouldering the majority of care responsibilities.

This can lead to resentment and strain on family relationships. For example, my brother and I, who lived closer to our parents, ended up taking on most of their daily needs. One of my siblings lived far away, so he was not able to contribute as much.

Resolution: Open communication is key. We held a family meeting where everyone expressed their feelings and concerns. We agreed to share responsibilities based on abilities and circumstances. My brother, who lives out of town, took on financial burdens and administrative tasks like managing bills and appointments. My other brother focused on daily physical care. And, because, as I mentioned in the previous chapter, my mother had taken out memory care insurance, we were actually able to hire a caregiver to sit with her simply to keep her company and feed her.

2. Financial Disputes: Money matters can cause severe tension. Arguments may arise about how to use parents' savings or how to share costs associated with their care. The tensions can run even higher if one family member strays from the wishes of the parents.

Resolution: In our case, we decided to consult a financial advisor. It helped to have an unbiased third-party perspective. We created a budget and set guidelines for expenditure. Everyone contributed according to their ability, and we made sure to use our parents' savings responsibly.

3. Decisions About Healthcare: This can be a contentious issue, especially when it comes to decisions about long-term care, medical treatments, or end-of-life plans.

Resolution: The voice of our parents was paramount. We involved them in discussions and considered their wishes first. Also, we sought advice from healthcare professionals to ensure we made informed decisions. It was challenging, but it taught us to respect and empathize with each other's viewpoints.

4. Disagreements About Living Arrangements: Some family members might prefer a nursing home for professional care, while others might want parents to stay home or move in with them. This is a topic for serious discussion, weighing the needs of your own family against the needs of your parent. Be sure to explore all options and discuss them with those who have been down this road.

Resolution: Weighing the pros and cons while keeping everyone's needs in mind helped us decide. As a family, we decided on long-term care for our parents because it is what worked best for us. This is one of those situations when every family will have unique challenges and issues to work out. My best advice, continue doing what is best for all involved.

5. Emotional Stress and Burnout: The emotional toll of caregiving can cause disputes among family members, often due to exhaustion and stress. A recent study showed caregivers are sleep deprived—36.7% reported getting terrible sleep since caring for their parents (Tesoro-Morioka, M.).

Resolution: Self-care is imperative. We learned to take

breaks, share caregiving tasks, and support each other emotionally. In some instances, seeking help from support groups or mental health professionals can be beneficial.

Keep in mind; these are just a few examples. Every family's situation is unique, and what worked for us might not work for you. The fundamental principle is empathy. Respect each other's feelings, perspectives, and capacities. Open, honest communication helps avoid misunderstandings. And remember, you're all working for the same goal: providing the best care for your loved ones. It's not an easy journey, but it's one that we tread out of love and respect for those who cared for us when we were helpless. Let that love guide your path.

Interactive Element

Here we are going to explore ways to practice your communication skills with your aging parents. Aging can be a daunting experience, and seniors often harbor apprehensions about the unknown, such as the loss of independence and the potential long-term effects of serious medical conditions. Consequently, these fears might contribute to their reluctance to seek assistance and their inclination to keep any new symptoms they experience a secret.

As we care for our aging parents, there will be difficult conversations that need to happen. I want to share some valuable insights about the decisions we make and how our approach can make a real difference. The way we express our opinion can have a profound impact on the situation at hand. To successfully navigate the challenges of managing conflict and finding the best path for your parents, it's important to embrace a supportive approach instead of a pushy one.

Consider the following suggestions for effective communication that can help you strike the right balance:

- **Persistence is key:** Don't expect to resolve everything in one conversation. Be patient, broach your concerns multiple times, and avoid overwhelming them with too much information at once.
- **Avoid power struggles:** Rather than giving ultimatums or arguing, Involve them in decision-making, validating their feelings and opinions.
- **Be sensitive:** Voice your concerns without criticism, focusing on your feelings and worries instead of accusing them of poor decision-making.
- **Timing is essential:** The most productive discussions occur when we're all relaxed and not under stress.
- **Maintain calm:** Expressing your concerns calmly and lovingly can reassure them that change is okay.
- **Seek external help:** It can be helpful to find a support network for yourself if you're feeling anxious or overwhelmed.
- **Spend quality time with them:** As they continue to age, you'll likely appreciate some extra attention.

- **Engage them in conversation:** Instead of lecturing, ask questions to involve them in discussions.
- **Propose solutions:** Address their concerns by doing research and establishing trust.
- **Highlight the benefits:** When suggesting an option like assisted living, focus on the positive aspects, such as social and recreational activities or no longer having to cook and clean!
- **Involve family members:** Share caregiving responsibilities with siblings or other family members, if possible. As mentioned above, keep that open communication flowing.
- **Enlist the help of friends:** Sometimes, they might be more receptive to advice from a friend or neighbor.
- **Consult their doctor:** If all else fails, share your concerns with their healthcare professional, whose advice they might respect.
- **Discuss potential consequences:** If they're determined to maintain their current lifestyle, calmly express the potential risks involved.
- **Respect their autonomy:** Sometimes, despite all your efforts, they may remain firm in their decisions. Remember that they are adults and have the right to make their own choices unless otherwise directed by a physician.
- **Try to comprehend their behavior:** Listen to what they're saying and what they

might not be expressing. They might resist change due to fear or anxiety. Have an honest conversation about emotions and feelings, allowing them to express themselves freely.

- **Accept the situation:** You can't force them to accept help or explore new options. Find a way to come to terms with the situation. It may just be a matter of letting them handle it until they ask for help.
- **Treat them as adults:** It's important to remember that they're still your parents, deserving respect and dignity. Empower them in conversations and decision-making processes.

As a woman in the sandwich generation, I understand firsthand the challenges and complexities of caring for aging parents while juggling a challenging work environment, raising kids and other responsibilities. Communicating with family during this journey is essential for ensuring the best care for our loved ones and maintaining our own well-being. By fostering open and honest conversations, actively listening to one another's concerns, and sharing responsibilities, we can form a united front and navigate this path together. Remember, we are not alone in this journey, and by building a strong support system within our family, we can find strength, comfort, and solutions when we need them most. In the next chapter, we will explore the process of finding and managing caregivers, exploring the different options available to us, and providing guidance on selecting the best care for our aging parents.

Chapter 5

How to Find and Manage Caregiver Resources

* * *

When you come to the end of your rope, tie a knot and hang on. —Franklin D. Roosevelt

Peer Spotlight: Andrew

Andrew, a 45-year-old guy, whom I met in a private Facebook group specifically for members caught in the sandwich generation. Yup, there really is a group for everything these days. Andrew finds himself faced with the responsibility of caring for both his aging father, Robert, and his own family. For the past three years, Andrew has been actively involved in providing care for his dad, who is in his late seventies and has been living with him since his mother's passing. However, the growing demands of caregiving and the need for long-term care have become increasingly challenging for him as he struggles to find a solution that ensures his father's safety and happiness.

Andrew has always shared a close bond with his father, Robert, a retired schoolteacher who dedicated his life to education and family. Following the passing of Andrew's mother, Robert's health started to decline, and he began experiencing memory loss and mobility issues. Recognizing the need for additional support, he stepped up to become his father's primary caregiver.

As the years passed, Andrew witnessed the toll caregiving took on his own personal life and family. Balancing the demands of his full-time job, raising two teenagers, and providing round-the-clock care for his father was becoming overwhelming. The physical and emotional strain on Andrew was evident, and he knew he needed to explore long-term care options for his father.

However, his greatest struggle was finding a care facility that would meet his needs while ensuring his happiness and quality of life. Robert was a fiercely independent man who cherished his routines and valued his freedom. Andrew was worried that transitioning his father to a care facility might disrupt his happiness and sense of autonomy.

Andrew embarked on a comprehensive search to find the perfect long-term care facility for his father. His criteria included safety, quality of care, and an environment that would promote his father's happiness and engagement. He consulted with healthcare professionals, toured various facilities, and sought recommendations from other families in similar situations.

Ultimately, Andrew found a reputable care facility that specialized in memory care. The place offered a warm and inviting environment, dedicated staff, and engaging activities tailored to the resident's interests. The facility also had stringent safety measures in place, ensuring Robert's well-being.

Understanding that the transition to a care facility might be difficult for Robert, Andrew took proactive steps to ensure his father's happiness during this challenging time. He involved Robert in the decision-making process, sharing his concerns and discussing the benefits of the care facility. Andrew emphasized that the move was intended to enhance Robert's safety, well-being, and social interactions with peers facing similar challenges.

To help Robert settle into his new environment, Andrew decorated his dad's room with familiar photos and mementos, ensuring a sense of familiarity. He also maintained regular visits, spending quality time with his dad and participating in the facility's activities together.

Over time, he noticed positive changes in his father's overall well-being. Robert adjusted to the care facility, formed meaningful connections with staff and residents, and regained a sense of purpose and engagement. Andrew witnessed his father's happiness and contentment, which alleviated his initial concerns and guilt associated with transitioning his care responsibilities to professionals.

By finding a care facility that prioritized both safety and happiness, Andrew successfully managed to balance his father's needs while taking care of his own family. The decision enabled him to reclaim some personal time and devote energy to his wife, children, and career while still maintaining an active role in his father's life.

Andrew's journey as a caregiver in the sandwich generation exemplifies the challenges and complexities faced by many individuals. By making an informed decision and prioritizing his father's safety and happiness, Andrew was able to find a suitable long-term care facility.

Types of Caregiver Resources

If you're currently taking care of an aging parent at home, you're likely assisting them with various activities such as bathing, dressing, transportation, and food preparation. On top of that, you may also have to handle legal and financial matters, such as making medical decisions and managing bills and budgets. Thankfully, there are several community care options available to provide support for both you and your loved one.

This information aims to give you an overview of the different services and programs that caregivers and individuals with cognitive disorders or chronic health conditions can access.

The first step in determining the best kind of help and support for your family is assessing your particular needs, values, and preferences. With the wide range of services available to caregivers, it's important to identify your specific concerns. It's also important to consider the values and preferences of your loved one regarding the type of help they are willing to accept. Holding a family meeting can be helpful in discussing care needs and making decisions.

Consider asking yourself the following questions and jotting down the answers:

- What kind of help does my loved one need at this moment to maintain as much independence as possible? (This can include nutrition services, dressing, bathing, lifting, medication management, supervision, companionship, housekeeping, and transportation.)
- What kinds of help might be required in the future?
- Who in the family will take the lead in caregiving and/or arranging care?
- How much financial resources are available to pay for outside assistance? Can insurance cover any services?
- Which days and times do I need help?
- What kind of assistance am I capable of providing myself?
- Does my job impact the amount of care I can provide?
- What types of help are my friends and family members willing to offer?
- Are we comfortable with having a stranger in our home to assist us?
- Do we require a caregiver of a specific gender?
- Are we considering out-of-home care? If so, what kind, how often, and for how long?

Community care programs and services vary across states, counties, and communities. Most areas now have support services specifically designed for individuals with Alzheimer's, stroke, Parkinson's, and other chronic health conditions. However, the availability of services and the eligibility requirements may differ in each community. The following section provides an overview of the main community care options for both the care recipient and their caregivers:

- **Informal care** involves the assistance of friends, family, religious communities, neighbors, and others who can share the responsibilities of caregiving. This informal support network can help with specific tasks, provide emotional support to you and your loved one, and help maintain a healthy level of social and recreational activity. Creating a list of your informal helpers' contact information will be a valuable source of support for routine assistance or in times of emergency.
- **Information and referral services** help you identify local resources. Caregiver Resource Centers, Area Agencies on Aging (AAAs), senior centers, and community mental health programs are all valuable resources that can help you find potential services such as adult daycare programs, respite care, and meal programs. Staff members in these organizations can provide information about service availability, whom to contact, eligibility requirements, and hours of operation.

- **Care management services** can help locate and, if needed, provide hands-on management of services for your loved one.

If you're in the sandwich generation, like me, and taking care of aging parents, you might be considering home care options to help your loved ones continue living independently at home. Home care combines health care and supportive services tailored to the needs of homebound individuals who are sick or disabled. The specific hours, services, and level of care provided will depend on the health condition of the care recipient and the caregiver's needs. In some cases, physician approval may be required. You can hire aides directly or through a staffing agency.

Home Care

There are two types of home care available: home health care services and non-medical home care services. Home health care services encompass a wide range of medical assistance, including medication management, nursing services, and physical therapy. Non-medical home care services, on the other hand, focus on providing companionship, housekeeping, cooking, and various household activities and chores.

The cost of home care varies based on the level of care required. Generally, non-medical home care attendants charge less than nurses who monitor the recipient's medical needs. It's important to shop around and compare fees. Medicare, Medicaid (MediCal in California), and some private insurance or long-term care policies may cover limited home healthcare services with certain restrictions. In other cases, you may need to pay out of pocket. Non-medical home care aides can be found through personal referrals or private home care agencies, hospitals, social service agencies, public health departments, nursing schools, and other community organizations.

Hospice Care

Hospice care provides specialized services to enhance the quality of life for terminally ill individuals by managing symptoms and preserving dignity until the end. A team of professionals and volunteers works together with the patient and family to address physical, psychological, social, and spiritual needs. They offer medical and nursing care, social services, dietary guidance, counseling, emotional support, and necessary equipment like hospital beds and wheelchairs.

Hospice care involves regularly scheduled visits and can also provide round-the-clock care when required. Generally, intrusive or "heroic" medical interventions are avoided based on the patient's preferences, and pain relief is a primary focus. Support for loved ones often extends into the bereavement period. Medicare, Medicaid, and most private insurance plans offer coverage for hospice care.

Support Groups

Caregiver support groups are gatherings where friends and family members come together regularly to share information and discuss practical solutions to common problems. These groups are an excellent source of information about available resources and provide caregivers with a chance to receive and offer encouragement, understanding, and support to others facing similar challenges. Connecting with other caregivers can significantly reduce stress. You can find support groups through hospitals, mental health programs, support organizations, or Alzheimer's Association chapters, and even online. *Family Caregiver Alliance* offers three online support groups.

Therapy

Employee assistance programs, if available in your workplace, can be a valuable benefit. The assistance provided can vary widely but typically includes counseling for personal issues like depression, stress, addiction, financial crises, and family illness or death. Some programs may also help with locating eldercare and childcare resources. Additionally, you may be eligible for paid or unpaid leave through federal, state, or employer-provided programs. It's worth reaching out to your human resources department for more information.

Plan Ahead

When it comes to contacting programs and care services, it's important to plan ahead and start looking for resources before the situation becomes overwhelming. Be prepared to make several phone calls or go through referrals to find the right program or person to assist you. If you have a care manager or health care provider who helped assess your needs, don't hesitate to ask for their help in finding resources. Take note of all the information you receive, including dates, names, phone numbers, websites, and decisions made. Be specific about your needs when dealing with agencies and assertive in advocating for what you require. Calling in the mornings is usually recommended. Ensure you understand the follow-up procedures and next steps before ending the call. Be aware that waiting lists may exist for certain services, but planning ahead can help minimize the waiting period. If fees are involved, ask for a rate sheet detailing the services provided for each fee. Be cautious when relying on "free" online referral services, as they may prioritize facilities that pay for listings rather than indicating the quality of care provided. Lastly, don't hesitate to ask for help. Many community agencies exist to provide services to individuals in need, and you have the right to access these services since they are often funded by taxes, contributions, or service fees. Remember that not everyone may fully understand the needs of caregivers, so educating professionals in the community may be necessary to obtain services successfully. Don't give up in your search for support and resources.

Managing the Costs

As a woman in the heart of my life, I have and am still chartering the waters of the so-called "sandwich generation," the group wedged between taking care of our aging parents and raising our own children. When you are thrown into the caregiver role for your parents, you soon understand the steep emotional, physical, and financial costs of caregiving.

It's like living in a state of perpetual motion, making sure everyone else is okay, sometimes forgetting to pause and take care of yourself.

The costs of caregiving are immense, and they're not limited to finance. There's a constant emotional toll, a slow drain on your physical health, and an unending need to be present for every crisis, large or small. But the financial aspect cannot be ignored. There are out-of-pocket costs for medical expenses, travel, home modifications, respite care, and the potential loss of income if one must cut back on work hours or quit a job altogether. You want to avoid watching your parent's savings dwindle as you may need to dip into them to cover the costs your parents' pensions and Medicare don't meet.

How to Cope

Coping with these costs has been a complex process. Initially, I was overwhelmed by the mounting bills and expenses. However, I sought advice from a financial planner who helped me create a budget and a plan. I found resources, like elder care financial assistance programs and tax breaks for caregivers, that I hadn't known existed. I also joined a local caregiver support group. There, I found a network of individuals facing the same struggles, and we've become a resource for each other, sharing tips, advice, and sometimes just a shoulder to cry on.

How to Save

Managing costs has been a significant part of my caregiving journey. I learned to scrutinize medical bills for errors, which are surprisingly common. I also found cost-saving measures like ordering generic prescriptions or getting medications through mail order, which often offer savings. I researched home care agencies extensively, learning to balance the cost with the level of care they could provide.

I also found ways to reduce financial costs. I've learned to be resourceful and frugal. For example, when my parents first began to show signs of mental decline, I started preparing home-cooked meals for them instead of relying on expensive meal delivery services. Additionally, I reached out to local community services that provide free or discounted services, such as transportation to medical appointments or senior centers offering activities to keep my parents engaged.

Financial Tools

In coping with these costs, I also made use of financial tools. I consulted with a tax professional to understand potential deductions for caregiving expenses. I explored long-term care insurance for my parents, which could help offset future costs. And I made sure to safeguard my own financial future by contributing to my retirement fund, even if it's a smaller amount than before.

After all the phone calls, interviews, and meticulous research, I can say that the process of finding and managing caregiver resources has its challenging moments, to say the least. We are always working on the tightrope of ensuring the best possible care for our parents while managing within our means. Despite the hurdles, every effort, and every struggle, is worth it to see our parents comfortable and cared for. Along the way, I've discovered that it's about so much more than just being organized and resourceful. It's about human connections, understanding, and compassion.

As we close this chapter, we look forward to a journey of a different sort—one that travels into the emotional terrain of caring for an aging parent and the necessity of supporting those who shoulder this responsibility.

As we step into the next chapter, we'll explore the emotional support required not only for our beloved parents but also for ourselves as caregivers. We might be their children, but we are also human, carrying a heavy weight of love, duty, and sometimes, guilt and grief. It's a complex, delicate dance but remember, as we take this journey together, that it's okay to lean on others and to seek solace and support. We're not alone in this, even if, at times, it may feel that way. It's okay to be you—the caregiver, the child, the human—with all the strength and frailty that it entails.

Scan the QR CODE to go directly to Amazon to review

Elizabeth Roth

Dear Reader,

✍ If you're finding this book helpful or enlightening, I warmly invite you to share your thoughts and experiences by leaving a review on Amazon, as your feedback is invaluable to both myself and future readers. Thank you! ✍

Head To Amazon To Write A Review

Scan the QR CODE to go directly to Amazon to review

Chapter 6

Emotional Support for Caregivers and Aging Parents

* * *

Every one of us needs to show how much we care for each other and, in the process, care for ourselves. —Princess Diana

Peer Spotlight: Isabella

Isabella is a 47-year-old woman, a single mother with two teenage children with whom I also connected within an online support group. It seemed fitting to share her story here because she has a huge understanding and a wealth of knowledge about the need for support for those caring for an aging loved one.

She is a full-time architect working for a renowned architectural firm in New Jersey. Besides her demanding job and role as a mother, she has become the primary caregiver for her 79-year-old father, who has recently been diagnosed with Parkinson's disease.

Isabella found herself in the classic sandwich generation situation, juggling her time and responsibilities between her children and her aging father, all while trying to manage her career. Her father's physical and mental health declined, and he was increasingly dependent on her. Isabella's friends were supportive but busy with their own lives, and she didn't have siblings to share the responsibilities. Isolation and burnout were creeping in.

Isabella's work productivity started declining. Her stress levels were skyrocketing, leading to sleepless nights. She started missing her children's school events and outings due to her father's frequent medical appointments. She often felt guilty and helpless, and a sense of despair started to take hold. Her social life was non-existent, as her father required round-the-clock care, and she was too exhausted to meet friends or participate in any activities.

After some particularly tough days, Isabella realized that she could not continue this way. She needed support. She began to research various resources available to caregivers. She started attending a local support group for people who were taking care of parents with Parkinson's disease, where she could share her feelings and learn from others' experiences.

Isabella reached out to a local agency on aging, who connected her with a social worker. The social worker helped her find in-home care support for her father, where a professional caregiver would come home for a few hours daily to take care of him, thus providing Isabella some respite.

She learned about the benefits of telehealth, which reduced the number of in-person medical appointments her father needed, thus freeing up some of her time. Her father's doctor also referred them to a Parkinson's disease specialist nurse, who helped with medication management and symptom control.

She also found online resources that provided her with information, education, and a sense of community.

Finally, Isabella contacted her human resources department at work to discuss her situation. They were understanding and agreed to a flexible work arrangement, allowing her to work from home twice a week.

Although Isabella's life is still full of challenges, these resources and changes have made a significant difference. She no longer feels isolated and has found a community of people who understand her struggles. Her stress levels have reduced, and she can devote quality time to her children again. She is also better equipped to care for her father, and the in-home caregiver's assistance has relieved her of the constant pressure. She has even found time to rekindle her social life.

Isabella's story is a testament to the power of seeking help and using available resources when dealing with the intense pressure of being part of the sandwich generation. The key is understanding that you cannot do it all alone and that reaching out for support can bring about positive change for both the caregiver and the ones they care for.

Understanding the Emotional Impact of Aging and Caregiving

When we are faced with taking care of our aging parents while balancing other life responsibilities, it can have a significant impact on your life. I wanted to include some points to consider:

Stress and emotional overload: As caregivers, we are frequently in high-demand situations, dealing with medical issues, logistical problems, and possibly even legal or financial issues. The constant demand often leads to chronic stress. I remember when I started having sleep problems, I was irritable and depressed. A recent study indicated that 36.7% of caregivers reported poor sleep (Tesoro-Morioka, M. (n.d). It is not uncommon to start noticing physical health issues like high blood pressure. You should know that 53% of caregivers will show a decline in their health (Tesoro-Morioka, M.(n.d). For instance, if your mother requires assistance throughout the night, this might disrupt your own sleep pattern leading to chronic fatigue and irritability.

Role reversal: I truly struggled with role reversal when I started caring for the person who once cared for me. Watching my once strong father and resilient mother decline wreaked havoc on my emotions. It is normal to start feeling a sense of loss as we grieve for the more independent parent we once knew.

Guilt and Anger: Have I been angry? Hell yes! Am I immediately flooded with guilt? That would be a resounding yes. Joining a support group and discovering just how normal these emotions are was helpful. I remember the first time I got truly angry. Life was coming at me like an avalanche, and I was just in a robotic state. Then, one day my mother insisted I drop what I was doing to bring her lotion. Simple enough, but on this day, I snapped. After screaming into the phone at her, reminding her how selfish this behavior was, I slammed the phone down and sobbed on my kitchen floor for the next thirty minutes. Flooded with guilt, I brought her the lotion only for her to ask what I was even doing there. It is okay to put yourself first; remember that.

Isolation and Loneliness: For those of us caring for our parents, we can feel like we are alone on a deserted island. While our friends and coworkers live a typical life, you can't begin to form the correct words to describe your own personal hell. Only those who are doing what you are will relate. Gone are the days of after-work cocktails or a nice dinner out with your partner. When all your free time is dedicated to your parent's care, your social life suffers, and you are lonely. To survive this, you need to acknowledge how important your life still is outside of being a caregiver.

Impact on Personal Goals and Relationships: Six months prior to my mother's dementia diagnosis, our family was planning the most amazing vacation. We were going to take most of the summer, rent an RV and see as many things as we could. It has been five years and we never took that trip. Putting your own life and plans on hold as a caregiver happens all the time. It was about this time I started arguing with my husband more, as he didn't seem to understand how much time I had to dedicate to my parents. Keeping those lines of communication open, seeing a therapist, and allowing myself to cry and feel all helped me get through.

Sense of Fulfillment: It is not all doom and gloom. Ensuring my parents were being well taken care of was important to me. They always went above and beyond taking care of me and my brothers, so despite our life turning upside down, I needed to do this. Don't be surprised if, among all your feelings, you also feel fulfilled.

The number one thing I want you to remember is it's normal to experience these emotions and impacts. It's imperative we seek support, whether from caregiver support groups, professional counselors, respite care services, or friends and family. Taking care of yourself is not a luxury but a necessity in this journey.

How to Reduce Isolation When Caregiving

Caring for our parents is an experience that's filled with angst. I was one of my father's caregivers prior to his passing–a role I took on with utmost dedication and love. However, it can also be a profoundly lonely and isolating experience. The long hours, the emotional toll, and the intense responsibility often make it difficult to maintain connections with the outside world.

It is not uncommon for us to feel this way, and here is a closer at why:

- **Lack of Time:** The sheer amount of time the caregiving role demands can be staggering. Your day may revolve around your parent's needs—preparing meals, managing medications, helping them bathe and dress, and driving them to numerous medical appointments. This means we often don't have time for social activities or hobbies. In essence, it feels like our world shrinks.

- **Emotional Burden:** The emotional weight of watching a loved one age and become more dependent can be devastating. It's difficult to express these feelings to others, and this inability to share our experiences often leaves us feeling emotionally cut off.
- **Misunderstanding From Others:** Many of our friends and family members don't understand the extent of the caregiving role. They often ask why we can't just hire someone to take care of our parents. What they don't understand is that it's not just about physical assistance; it's about being there for them emotionally, which is a job that only a family member can truly fulfill.
- **Changes in Relationship Dynamics:** As my father's health declined, our relationship changed. I was no longer just his daughter; I was also his caregiver. This shift can often lead to feelings of loneliness as we navigate these new waters.

The next question is how we can, as caregivers, reduce feelings of isolation and loneliness. Here are some suggestions:

- **Join Support Groups:** Participating in caregiver support groups can be very helpful. These groups offer a space where I can share my experiences, challenges, and emotions with people who understand what I'm going through.

I remember attending my first caregiver support meeting; it was such a relief to find a community that knew exactly what I was experiencing. If you do one thing, join a group, it will help so much.

- **Seek Help:** It's essential to ask for help and delegate tasks when possible. I often reached out to my brothers to help with Dad's doctor appointments and so forth. Don't hesitate to hire some extra help if your parents are still at home. This not only gives us a breather but also provides opportunities to engage in social activities or get some rest.
- **Self-Care:** This can't be stressed enough. Taking time out for myself was essential to avoid burnout. It could be something as simple as a 15-minute walk around the block or a quiet cup of coffee in the morning before the day's duties start. Take that time for yourselves because that burnout sneaks up on us fast!
- **Use Technology:** To help stay connected with friends and family, lean on those video calls. This gives you a chance to feel involved in their lives still, and catching up is always great for the soul. It also provides a sense of normalcy in our otherwise care-centered routine.
- **Counseling:** It's okay to seek professional help. Seeing a therapist has helped me cope with my feelings of isolation and loneliness. In our family, it was actually one of my brothers who

reached out to a therapist first. I was proud of him for ignoring the stigma society places on men in therapy and doing what he needed. Therapy should provide a safe space to express your worries, fears, and frustrations without judgment.

Caregiving is a marathon, not a sprint. It's essential to keep connections alive, reach out for support, and, most importantly, take care of yourself while caring for your loved one. Being aware of my own needs and addressing them has made me a more patient and resilient caregiver.

How to Provide Emotional Support for Aging Parents

As someone who has been a caregiver for her parents, the experience is both deeply personal and universally relatable for many people in my situation.

The importance of providing emotional support for our elderly parents can't be overstated. Just as we cater to their physical needs, ensuring their emotional well-being is essential as they navigate the twilight of their lives. Our parents, who once were our caretakers, find themselves in a vulnerable stage where they may feel isolated, anxious, or even scared. This is where our role as their emotional support system comes in.

Meeting your parents' emotional needs involves multiple dimensions. It's about recognizing their emotions, being there to comfort them, and sometimes, just being present. These are people who have seen the world and lived through countless experiences, and they hold a vast ocean of feelings that often remain unexpressed.

One of the ways you can meet their emotional needs is through communication. Regular, open, and honest conversations can provide a platform for them to voice their thoughts, fears, or concerns. For example, my father, who was a once-vibrant and independent man, would start to grapple with the loss of mobility and cognitive abilities. Instead of dismissing his frustration, I would engage him in conversations about his feelings. I would encourage him to express his emotions, validating them and reminding him it's okay to feel this way.

Another way to provide emotional support is to ensure they still feel valued and purposeful. Our elderly parents often struggle with a loss of identity as they retire from work or can't engage in activities they once loved. By involving them in simple decisions around the house or seeking their advice on matters, you can give them a sense of importance and purpose. For instance, my father loved gardening but met a time when he could no longer actively participate due to his physical constraints. So, I used to ask him for tips and suggestions while I did the gardening. His eyes would light up with a sense of purpose when he saw his advice being put into action.

Moreover, providing them with companionship is an effective way to offer emotional support. Sometimes they don't need words; they just need someone to be there, someone to share their silence with. I would often sit with my father, enjoying a peaceful sunset or listening to his favorite music. These moments of shared companionship convey a message louder than words, a message that says, "You are not alone."

But remember, it's also important to encourage independence where possible. Overdoing help can sometimes lead them to feel helpless. Allow them to perform tasks they are capable of, even if they're slower at it. This way, they maintain a sense of control over their lives, boosting their emotional well-being.

Caring for aging parents is a journey that requires patience, compassion, and resilience. In their smiles, in their peace, you find an unmatched sense of fulfillment. As caregivers, it is our responsibility and privilege to provide them with the emotional support they need, helping them live their golden years with dignity and grace.

How to Find Emotional Support as a Caregiver

Let's talk first about the emotional challenges of caregiving because there is a lot of guilt and worry that comes with caregiving. When I was with my father, I often felt guilty about the time I'm not spending with my children. When I was with my kids, guilt crept in because I felt like I was neglecting my dad. Then there's the worry; is my dad happy? Are my kids eating well when I'm not around?

This constant push and pull often result in an overwhelming feeling of exhaustion. I remember times when I was so fatigued I could barely keep my eyes open. And amid all this, it's easy to lose sight of who you are. It's easy to forget about self-care when your days and nights revolve around caring for others.

Those are just some of the emotional challenges, but it's not all doom and gloom. Despite the difficulties, there are ways to find emotional support when caregiving. Below, you will find some of what worked for me:

- **Acknowledge the situation:** It's okay to say it's hard, it's okay to feel overwhelmed, and it's okay to need help. Often, we put on a brave face, trying to do everything ourselves, but it's important to remember that support will keep everyone healthier.
- **Find your people:** I joined a local caregiver support group, and it's there that I found people who understood exactly what I was going through. We shared our challenges, cried together, and also shared tips and tricks on how to navigate through our caregiving roles. There's something incredibly comforting about being around people who understand your situation, and it's helped me feel less alone.
- **Normalize therapy:** I sought therapy when the emotional burden got too heavy to carry on my own. As I mentioned earlier, my brother embraced therapy as well. Speaking to a mental health professional gives us the tools to deal with stress and anxiety better, and it also offers a safe space to vent and express our feelings without judgment.
- **Communicate:** I talked to my kids about the situation, and you'd be surprised at how

understanding they can be. We became a team, helping each other out. I found comfort in their resilience and their unwavering love and support.
- **Self-care:** I know this seems like a common theme throughout the book, but that is only because of how critical it is. Find some time each day, even if it's just a few minutes, to do something that brings you joy or peace. For me, it's my early morning walks. They give me a chance to clear my head, breathe, and prepare for the day.

Caregiving is emotionally challenging; there's no sugar-coating it. But remember, there are resources out there to help, and you don't have to do this alone. It's okay to ask for help. It's okay to take care of yourself. And above all, it's okay to acknowledge your feelings. It doesn't make you any less devoted or loving—it makes you human.

Wrapping up this chapter, we discovered that navigating the intricate world of finding help and resources for both yourself and your aging parents is no small feat. However, armed with the knowledge and resources gathered throughout this chapter, I hope you are better equipped to face the challenges head-on. As we jump into the next chapter on balancing a career and caregiving, we will explore strategies and insights that will empower you to create a harmonious equilibrium between your professional aspirations and the invaluable role you play in your parents' lives.

Chapter 7

Balancing Work and Caregiver Responsibilities

* * *

Compassion automatically invites you to relate with people because you no longer regard people as a drain on your energy.— Chogyam Trungpa

Peer Spotlight: Josh

Meet Josh. He is a 45-year-old marketing manager working in a mid-sized firm in Chicago. His wife, Julie, a former colleague of mine, works full-time as well, and they have two teenage children. When I reached out to Josh's wife recently to catch up, she knew he would want to share his story in my book. Sometimes sharing your experience can be therapeutic.

Josh's father passed away a few years ago, and his only sibling lives overseas, making him the primary caregiver for his mother. Once his dad passed, his 82-year-old mother,

Mary, moved in with their family. Unfortunately, his mom is showing early signs of dementia.

Caring for an aging parent, especially one with health issues, is physically and emotionally exhausting. Josh told me he often finds himself waking up in the middle of the night to find his mother wandering aimlessly around the house, in turn compromising not only his sleep and overall well-being but his wife and kids' too. He is also experiencing feelings of guilt and anxiety as he struggles to balance his career and the needs of his mother.

Josh told me all about his struggle to find time to manage his professional responsibilities, his mother's doctor appointments, and the needs of his own family. His work performance is starting to decline, and he is falling behind on his responsibilities at home.

The cost of his mother's medications, in-home care, and regular medical checkups is putting a significant financial strain on his family. He is constantly worried about how to fund his mother's escalating healthcare needs and manage his own family's finances.

Josh has set a meeting with his boss about his situation. Companies often have policies to support employees facing family health crises, such as flexible working hours, the ability to work from home, or even a leave of absence if necessary.

Josh has been advised to look into local caregiver support services. Many communities offer resources like adult day care, respite care, meal delivery services, and caregiver support groups. These services can help lighten his load and provide emotional support.

Hiring a professional caregiver for a few hours a day or a

few days a week can give Josh some respite and help ensure that his mother's needs are met when he is at work. He may also want to consider a live-in caregiver, depending on his mother's condition and the family's financial situation.

Josh also met with a financial planner and an eldercare lawyer to understand the best ways to manage his mother's healthcare costs. He is going to explore Medicaid, which provides health coverage for some low-income individuals, including some low-income adults and people with certain disabilities.

Josh's situation illustrates the significant challenges faced by those trying to balance work and caregiving responsibilities. However, by implementing these solutions, individuals like Josh can find a more manageable balance between work, caregiving, and personal health. It also underscores the importance of companies providing support to employees who are caregivers, as their number is likely to increase in the coming years.

Challenges We Face Balancing Work and Caregiving

The challenges of balancing work, caregiving, and personal needs can be enormous. I wanted to discuss several key challenges I faced and provide examples for each point.

> ***Time Management:*** This is one of the most significant challenges. Caring for an elderly parent can be very time-consuming, often unpredictable, and it is difficult to fit in around a full-time job. This is especially true if the parent's health is deterio-

rating and they require more constant care. For example, I remember times when my father's health took a sudden downturn, and he would be rushed to the hospital, often in the middle of a workday. I found myself juggling students and grading with emergency room visits simultaneously, feeling torn between my responsibilities.

Financial Pressure: The costs associated with caregiving, such as medical bills, medication, home care services, or home modifications, can put a considerable financial burden on the caregiver, especially when also supporting children. Balancing the costs of my children's education, extracurriculars, and my father's increasing medical expenses was a constant financial tightrope.

Emotional Stress: Caring for an ailing parent can be emotionally taxing, potentially leading to caregiver burnout. On top of this, you may also experience guilt, worry, or sadness related to their decline in health. There were times when the emotional strain of seeing my father's health decline, coupled with the everyday stress of work and raising children, felt suffocating. It's not easy seeing a loved one suffer and feel unable to change their situation.

Physical Health Impact: The stress and physical demands of caregiving can have a serious impact on your own health, often leading to sleep deprivation, lack of exercise, and neglecting personal healthcare needs. In the effort to manage my father's health, my children's schedules, and work deadlines, I frequently neglected my own health, skipping meals or regular health checkups and not getting enough sleep.

Workplace Discrimination or Penalties: Despite legal protections, some caregivers experience workplace discrimination or penalties due to their caregiving responsibilities. They may face decreased work opportunities, inflexibility, or even job loss. At times, I sensed my coworkers and my department head were frustrated with my frequent need for time off. I even had to ask a fellow coworker to cover classes on multiple occasions.

Lack of Personal Time: Between caregiving, work, and parenting, it's easy to neglect personal needs, hobbies, or social activities. This can lead to feelings of isolation and loss of identity outside of being a caregiver. I had little to no time for myself, and even when I did, I was too exhausted to enjoy it. My hobbies and social life took a backseat to my responsibilities.

By recognizing these challenges and seeking support when needed, it can become more manageable. It's essential to remember to take care of your health and emotional well-being during this period.

Helpful Strategies

Taking on the role of caregiver for an aging parent or loved one while also managing your own career and family responsibilities can be considered a Herculean feat. But there are strategies you can employ to make this sandwich generation situation more manageable. Below are several tips, each explained and accompanied by examples.

> ***Communicate Openly and Regularly:*** Share your situation with your employer and coworkers. You might be surprised how understanding they can be, and they might be able to offer flexibility in your working hours or the option to work remotely. For example, if your mother needs to attend regular medical appointments, you could arrange to start work earlier and leave earlier to accompany her.
>
> ***Create a Routine:*** Establish a predictable daily routine to provide structure for both you and your parents. Consistent routines can decrease anxiety and improve the quality of sleep. For example, having a set mealtime, medication time, and leisure activities can add structure to both of your lives and create a more balanced schedule.
>
> ***Prioritize and Organize:*** Establishing priorities is crucial when managing multiple responsibilities. Create a comprehensive schedule that includes both work and caregiving tasks. Identify critical tasks and

allocate dedicated time for them. Use tools like calendars, task lists, or mobile apps to stay organized. By setting priorities, you can ensure that essential tasks are completed on time.

Delegate and Ask for Help: You don't have to do everything yourself. If possible, delegate tasks among family members and friends, or hire professional help. For example, if you have siblings, you could create a caregiving schedule so each of you has specific days to care for your parent. Or hire a professional caregiver for a few hours each day to give yourself a break.

Set Boundaries: Establish boundaries to maintain a healthy work-life balance. Clearly communicate your availability and limitations to both your employer and family members. Avoid overextending yourself by saying yes to every request. Learn to say no when necessary to protect your own well-being and prevent burnout.

Take Advantage of Employer Benefits: Familiarize yourself with your company's employee benefits and policies. Many employers offer assistance programs, flexible work arrangements, or paid leave options for caregivers. Utilize these benefits to support your caregiving responsibilities without compromising your career.

How to Communicate With Your Employer

Life has thrown some insane curve balls your way. You are smack in the middle of caring for an aging parent just at the height of your career. It is as if someone slammed on the brakes and insisted on a different destination. When it comes to communicating with your employer about your caregiving responsibilities, try some of these steps I personally used.

1. Understand Your Situation: Before you approach your employer, ensure you have a clear understanding of your responsibilities as a caregiver. Know how much time it will take, what specific tasks you'll be doing, and how it may affect your ability to do your job. Be prepared to provide a realistic estimate of the commitment involved.

2. Prepare Your Case: Document the impact of your caregiving responsibilities on your work. This could be specific instances when you had to leave early, come in late, or were unable to complete tasks. Show how your productivity may be affected. This documentation will provide a solid basis for your conversation.

3. Research Company Policies: Investigate your company's policies related to caregiving, family leave, flexible work schedules, or working from home. Understanding these policies will help you know what accommodations you may be able to ask for. Also, be aware of any legal protections in your jurisdiction, such as the Family and Medical Leave Act (FMLA) in the United States.

4. Plan the Conversation: Decide when and where to have the discussion. It's usually best to schedule a formal meeting rather than trying to discuss it informally or in passing. This shows respect for your employer's time and highlights the seriousness of the issue.

5. Be Honest and Clear: During the conversation, be open about your situation and your need for flexibility. Explain your caregiving responsibilities and how they're affecting your work. Be clear about what you need from your employer in terms of support or accommodation.

6. Propose Solutions: Rather than just presenting the problem, come up with potential solutions. This might include a flexible work schedule, remote work, job sharing, or adjusting your responsibilities. This shows your initiative and commitment to your job.

7. Show Appreciation and Commitment: Express gratitude for your employer's understanding and patience. Reinforce your commitment to the company and your job. Show that you're trying to balance your responsibilities in a way that minimizes the impact on your work.

8. Follow Up in Writing: After the conversation, send an email summarizing what was discussed and agreed upon. This helps ensure everyone is on the same page and creates a record of the conversation.

9. Keep Communication Open: After your initial conversation, continue to keep your employer updated on your situation. This ongoing communication can help address issues before they become major problems.

Each employer and situation is different, and what works best in one situation may not be the best approach in another. The key is to be honest, respectful, and proactive in addressing the issue.

You likely turn off your laptop, and a wave of exhaustion washes over you, both physically and emotionally. Balancing the demands of your career with the increasing responsibilities of caring for your aging parent has taken its toll. You have most certainly questioned if you could continue on this path without jeopardizing your well-being.

Little did you know that the journey you were about to embark upon would lead to a profound understanding of caregiver stress and burnout. In the next chapter, we will come face-to-face with the harsh realities of neglecting self-care and learn invaluable lessons on how to preserve our strength while nurturing the ones we love.

Chapter 8

Coping Strategies for Stress and Burnout

* * *

Do what you can, with what you have, where you are.
—Theodore Roosevelt

Peer Spotlight: Emily and Sarah

Two sisters, who I met in a support group a while back, find themselves deeply entangled in the challenging task of caring for their aging parents. Over the years, the sisters have selflessly been devoted to their parents' well-being, resulting in signs of caregiver burnout. This narrative explores the pivotal moment when one sister, Sarah, takes a stand and insists on prioritizing self-care, thereby transforming their caregiving journey.

Emily and Sarah, both in their late 40s, have been diligently caring for their aging parents, Mr. and Mrs. Johnson, for the past five years. Their parents, once independent and real go-getters, have gradually become dependent due to age-related illnesses and mobility issues. The sisters initially shared the caregiving responsibilities, balancing their own families and careers with the needs of their parents.

As time passed, the weight of their caregiving duties began taking a toll on Emily and Sarah. Both sisters began exhibiting signs of caregiver burnout, including exhaustion, emotional distress, neglecting their own health, strained relationships, and decreased job performance. The constant demands and stress associated with caregiving were overshadowing their own well-being.

One evening, after a particularly challenging day, Sarah realized that their current approach was unsustainable. Overwhelmed and emotionally drained, she decided to take a stand for her own well-being and that of her sister. She invited Emily over for a heart-to-heart conversation, acknowledging the burnout they were experiencing and the urgent need for change.

During their conversation, Sarah expressed her concerns and shared her realization that they had neglected themselves in their commitment to caring for their parents. She stressed the importance of prioritizing self-care to ensure they could continue providing the best care for their parents without sacrificing their own physical and mental health.

Together, Emily and Sarah embarked on developing a new care plan that involved seeking external support and redefining boundaries. They enlisted the help of professional caregivers who could assist with specific tasks and provide respite care, allowing the sisters to take regular breaks. They also explored support groups, counseling services, and community resources to alleviate the emotional burden they had been carrying alone.

Sarah and Emily recognized the significance of self-care and actively incorporated practices into their daily routines. They committed to regular exercise, proper nutrition, and sufficient rest. They also designated specific "me-time" for hobbies, relaxation, and social activities. By consciously practicing self-care, they regained a sense of balance and control over their lives, enhancing their overall well-being.

As the girls began prioritizing self-care, positive changes started to emerge. Their energy levels increased, they became more present during caregiving, and their relationship improved. They experienced reduced stress levels and gained a renewed sense of purpose in their caregiving journey. By demanding better care for themselves, they inadvertently improved their ability to care for their parents.

The story of Emily and Sarah demonstrates the struggles faced by many caregivers and the importance of recognizing and addressing caregiver burnout. Sarah's decision to demand better care for herself and her sister became a turning point in their journey. By implementing self-care practices and seeking external support, they not only transformed their own well-being but also enhanced their ability to provide quality care for their aging parents. Their situation serves as a reminder that caring for oneself is essential when caring for others.

Understanding Caregiver Stress and Burnout

Caring Hearts: Positive Affirmations for Caregivers

I understand the struggle more than anyone. For years, I helped care for my aging parents–a labor of love that often went unnoticed and under-appreciated. From managing their medications and meals to assisting them with day-to-day activities, I was deeply entrenched in their lives. There was an ever-present fear that I was doing something wrong, that my efforts were inadequate. I would lie awake at night, thinking about all the tasks for the next day, the medical appointments, the constant monitoring, and the potential emergencies. My life was submerged in a relentless cycle of worry, fatigue, and responsibility. I was physically tired but, more than that, emotionally and mentally exhausted.

This, my friends, is caregiver stress, and it's a heavy burden to bear. You're so consumed with taking care of another that you forget to take care of yourself. The constant demands can make you feel alone, anxious, exhausted, and depressed. It doesn't come immediately, but over time, chronic stress can lead to a more serious problem, caregiver burnout. This is when you feel emotionally, physically, and mentally exhausted to the point where you are unable to cope with everyday activities. It feels as if you're running on empty, with no end in sight. I didn't realize it at the time, but my irritability, loss of interest in activities I used to enjoy, and a constant feeling of exhaustion were all signs I was burnt out. It's important to remember that caring for yourself is just as important as caring for others.

Why Are We Stressed and Burnt Out?

Looking back on the time I spent caring for my parents, I can attest to the physical, emotional, and mental toll it can have. It was one of the most punishing times in my life. Being a caregiver can be incredibly stressful and lead to burnout if not managed carefully. I wanted to offer some of the main reasons behind caregiver stress and burnout, along with examples from my own journey.

- **Emotional Demand**: The process of seeing your loved one's age and health deteriorate can take your breath away and leave you anxious. You may experience feelings of sadness, frustration, and even anger. It's a constant emotional weight, like a stone sitting heavy in your heart. For me, it was seeing my mother struggle to remember our faces due to cognitive decline. It was heartbreaking and emotionally exhausting.
- **Physical Strain**: Taking care of aging parents often involves physically demanding tasks. You might have to assist with moving them, dressing them, or other daily tasks. For instance, maybe your mother needs help with everything from getting out of bed to taking a bath. You will find

yourself constantly on your feet, and it is a physical challenge we often don't anticipate.

- **Lack of Personal Time**: As a caregiver, it's easy to feel like you've lost your personal life. Between taking care of your loved one and dealing with your own responsibilities, you may find that there's little to no time left for yourself. I remember days when I didn't even have time to sit down and have a cup of coffee.
- **Feeling Overwhelmed**: There are many aspects to caregiving, from managing medications to coordinating with specialists to handling financial matters. It can be overwhelming, and the pressure to do everything perfectly is a constant stressor. When my parents' health started to decline, the number of decisions I had to make daily seemed to multiply.
- **Financial Pressure**: The costs of caregiving can add up quickly and lead to financial stress. You may have to cut back on work hours or even quit your job to provide care. Additionally, out-of-pocket medical expenses can strain your budget. I had to balance my work with caregiving duties, which led to a reduction in income. Coupled with increased medical expenses, financial pressure was a significant stressor.
- **Social Isolation**: Caregiving is lonely, and I wish someone had prepared me for that. While

your friends are out living a life filled with traveling and exploring, you dream of a life you had similarly planned. If you try and explain this to anyone who hasn't lived it, they give you that pitiful smile and throw a positive mantra in your face. I often felt alone, missing out on social events because I was tied up with caregiving responsibilities. It is best to understand now that there will be school recitals, spelling bees, birthday parties, and more that you will miss because of your obligation to your parents.

- **Guilt**: We have talked about the feeling of guilt previously, but it is so important to understand how normal this is as a caregiver. You might feel guilty for feeling frustrated, for not doing enough, or even for wanting some time for yourself. I experienced guilt on several occasions, especially when I felt impatient with my parents.
- **Balancing it All**: As women, we do believe we can do it all. When you become sandwiched with your parent's care while still caring for your own family, it isn't possible to pull it all off. I need you to understand that it is okay. It is okay to take a breath, put your feet up, miss soccer practice, or take a day off from visiting your parents. Trying to do it all will have you burnt out faster than ever.

Self-Care Tips for Caregivers

If you are anything like me, you will be stressed and burnt out far before you admit it. I had those closest to me confiding in their worry. They were concerned how much weight I had lost, they wanted to know if I was eating. Little did they know I was lucky to grab a muffin on my way out the door each day. I would leave work and head straight to visit my parents. Getting home by 8:00 p.m. left me falling into bed rather than focusing on a balanced meal. To all caregivers reading this, remember you can't pour from an empty cup. Taking care of yourself is not a luxury but a necessity. Here are some self-care tips that helped me in my journey and could help you too.

- **Set boundaries**: Learn to say 'no' when you need to. It's important to recognize that there are limits to what you can provide. There will be things you cannot change, and it's okay to accept that. For instance, I stopped feeling guilty about not being able to attend all of my friends' social events.
- **Seek support**: Remember, it's okay to ask for help. Engage other family members in caregiving or consider hiring professional help if possible. I was initially hesitant but eventually found a local caregiver support group which was immensely helpful.
- **Maintain a healthy lifestyle**: Prioritize a balanced diet, regular physical activity, and

adequate sleep. Small changes, like going for a 10-minute walk around the block or choosing whole grains and fresh vegetables, helped me maintain my energy levels.

- **Practice mindfulness**: Engaging in mindful activities such as meditation, yoga, or even just quiet reflection can be incredibly beneficial. It helped me stay focused, reduced my anxiety, and improved my overall well-being.
- **Take breaks**: It's essential to have breaks to recharge. Schedule short breaks throughout the day and plan for a longer break every few months. Respite care services can step in to provide temporary relief. I recall hiring a professional caregiver for a week while I went on a short vacation. It was rejuvenating.
- **Stay connected**: Keep in touch with your friends and maintain your social life as much as possible. Being socially active can help alleviate feelings of isolation and provide a much-needed distraction. Regular catch-ups over coffee with my friends were my lifeline.
- **Plan your day**: Effective time management can significantly reduce stress. Try to organize your day and week ahead, leaving some wiggle room for unexpected tasks or events. I used to keep a diary to plan and track my tasks, which helped me stay organized and less stressed.
- **Celebrate small victories**: Taking care of an aging parent can be overwhelming, but

it's also filled with moments of joy. Celebrate those. Each day my father remembered my name or my mother could eat without assistance, I considered it a victory.

Remember, self-care isn't selfish; it's crucial. And it's not a one-size-fits-all. Explore and find what works best for you. Keep in mind that you're doing the best you can in a challenging situation, so be gentle with yourself.

How to Build Your Own Support System

Don't be like most of us and convince yourself you can do this without help. Oftentimes, our parents can raise a fuss because they aren't keen on having strangers care for them. This is understandable, but if they are not able to think about your needs, you have to.

Reflecting on my journey as a caregiver for my parents, I cannot overstate the importance of having a solid support system. Being a caregiver can feel isolating at times, but knowing that you have people you can lean on, who can provide advice, help, or just lend an empathetic ear can make a world of difference.

The Importance of a Support System

- **Emotional Support**: The emotional demands of caregiving can be unexplainable at times. A support system provides a safe space to express your feelings without judgment or guilt. They understand what you're going through and provide comfort, encouragement, and reassurance. There were times when I felt helpless and frustrated, but sharing my feelings with those in my support system helped lighten the emotional burden.

- **Sharing Responsibilities**: Caregiving can be physically and mentally exhausting. Having others who can share in the caregiving responsibilities, even in small ways, can provide much-needed respite. I was fortunate to have brothers who helped take care of our parents, providing me with time to rest and recharge.
- **Information and Resources**: A support system can provide valuable information and resources to better manage caregiving. They can help navigate complex healthcare systems, identify community resources, or share advice from their experiences. I received guidance on managing my parents' issues from a fellow caregiver in my support group. They can prove to be a valuable source of information.
- **Promoting Self-Care**: Your support system can remind you to take care of yourself and help you carve out time for self-care. They can step in to provide care, allowing you to take breaks and engage in activities that help reduce stress and maintain your physical and mental health. I am not exaggerating when three friends once

asked how they could help. I allocated grocery shopping to one, laundry to the other, and cooking family meals twice a week to the last. It took me three years of burnout before I realized how my people truly did want to help. They just needed me to tell them how to best do just that.

Building Your Support System

Now that I have attempted to show you just how much you need help let's discuss how to build that support system.

- **Involve Family Members:** If possible, involve your family members in the caregiving process. Hold a family meeting to discuss the needs of your aging parents and how each person can contribute. Not everyone may be able to provide direct care, but there are other ways to help, such as taking care of finances or groceries.
- **Join Support Groups:** Look for caregiver support groups in your community or online. These are great places to connect with others going through similar experiences. The insights and experiences shared by others can be very beneficial. I found solace and invaluable advice in a local support group.
- **Reach Out to Friends:** Don't hesitate to reach out to your friends. Let them know about your situation and the challenges you're facing.

They may not be able to provide direct help, but their emotional support can be invaluable. You don't have to travel this road alone.
- **Utilize Professional Resources:** Social workers, nurses, and doctors can all be part of your support system. They can provide professional advice and direct you to resources that can help. I regularly consulted with my parents' doctors and nurses, who provided me with practical tips and guidance.
- **Community Resources:** Investigate community resources available for caregivers. This can include respite care services, and meal delivery services, among others. These resources can provide practical assistance, giving you more time for self-care.
- **Hire Help:** If you decide to care for your parents at home, consider hiring help. Professional caregivers can provide services ranging from a few hours a week to full-time care, allowing you to have regular breaks.

Building a support system is necessary to avoid burnout and stress. Establishing a core group that can support you is a smart, proactive move to ensure you're not alone in this journey. It's not only beneficial for you but also for your aging parents, who will receive well-rounded care.

I am a firm believer that those of us who care for our senior parents have no idea of what we are getting into. It all happens so fast, and before you know it, you are selling their home and getting quotes for wheelchair ramps for your home. The issue is nobody sits us down and tells us how long this process could be. Maybe we think it will be a year or two, right? Wrong. You could be setting yourself up to care for your parents for the next ten years or more.

If this is a decision you are swimming in currently, you need your support system. This community— including family, friends, professional caregivers, and support groups— not only lightens the caregiving load but also contributes to the emotional well-being of the caregiver, enhancing resilience in the face of inevitable difficulties. It provides a circle of comfort, an ecosystem of empathy that enables us to sustain our spirits even as we navigate the complex terrain of caregiving. As we conclude this chapter, it's clear that having a sturdy support system in place is a cornerstone of effective caregiving. However, the journey does not stop here. Looking forward, we must strategically plan for the future to ensure both we, as caregivers, and our loved ones are properly taken care of. The following chapter will guide you through important considerations and decisions, preparing you for this next phase in your life after your loved one passes.

Chapter 9

Planning for the Future—Taking Care of Yourself and Your Loved Ones

* * *

The best years of your life are the ones in which you decide your problems are your own. You do not blame them on your mother, the ecology, or the president. You realize that you control your own destiny. — Albert Ellis

Peer Spotlight: David

A 52-year-old accountant whom I have known since he started doing my taxes 20 years ago has dedicated the last eight years of his life to taking care of his mother, Helen, who was suffering from dementia. I am thankful he wanted to share his story. Being an only child and without a family of his own, David was committed to providing the best care possible for his mother.

With the help of a part-time professional caregiver, he managed to balance his job with caregiving responsibilities.

Despite the considerable stress, he found purpose and fulfillment in caring for his mother. He felt that his world revolved around her and her needs.

However, when Helen passed away recently, David found himself lost in the emptiness of his house and his daily schedule. Struggling with grief and the abrupt halt of his caregiving duties, he grappled with the guilt of feeling relieved about no longer having to manage the constant anxiety and stress related to his mother's health.

The first step in his healing journey was acknowledging his grief. He needed to mourn his mother's passing and deal with his emotions healthily. His grief counselor encouraged him to take his time and openly express his feelings.

David also confronted his guilt. He realized his feeling of relief was not about his mother's passing but about the end of her suffering and the constant worry he lived with daily. Recognizing this was crucial for him to start overcoming his guilt.

After initial sessions with his counselor, he was encouraged to join a local support group for individuals who had lost a loved one to dementia. Connecting with people who had undergone similar experiences was therapeutic for him. He felt less alone and began to share his feelings more openly, without fear of judgment.

In the following months, David worked on redefining his identity beyond being a caregiver. He started by revisiting hobbies he'd abandoned during his caregiving years, like reading, hiking, and painting. He joined a book club and an art class, which helped him socialize and find a new purpose.

He also engaged in volunteer work at a local dementia care center. He realized that his personal experiences were invaluable and could provide comfort and guidance to others dealing with dementia in their loved ones. While it was challenging initially, it proved to be therapeutic, giving him a sense of purpose and connection.

He continued attending therapy sessions, focusing on self-compassion and mindfulness. He learned to practice gratitude, focusing on the positive aspects of his life.

Eventually, David decided to return to his full-time job as an accountant. The routine and mental stimulation benefited his recovery, and his colleagues provided a supportive environment.

His journey of healing was not linear; he had ups and downs. However, he continued moving forward, leaning on his support system, continuing therapy, and maintaining his rediscovered hobbies and volunteer work.

David's experience emphasizes that life after intensive caregiving can feel like walking through Jell-O wearing cement shoes. However, with the right support, self-compassion, and time, it's possible to navigate grief, overcome guilt, and reinvent one's life. By acknowledging his feelings and seeking help, he managed to transition from a devoted caregiver to a man rediscovering his worth and identity.

The End

The reality is that you will grieve forever. You will not "get over" the loss of a loved one; you will learn to live with it. You will heal and you will rebuild yourself around the loss you have suffered. You will be whole again but you will never be the same. Nor should you be the same nor would you want to.

— Elisabeth Kubler-Ross

It's a sobering reality that nobody prepares you for. The day when you've poured so much of yourself into caring for your aging parents, only to find that you now face a future without them. It's a peculiar sensation, like standing on the edge of a precipice, knowing you must leap but fearing what the freefall might feel like.

My situation was as follows. I had both parents residing in nursing homes for cognitive decline, dementia, and Alzheimer's. I lost my father in February of this year. My mother remains in care to this day. Every day was a delicate dance of ensuring their needs were met, tending to medical issues, and dealing with the subtle changes that come with aging. The roles were reversed; I became the parent, and they became the child. It was a role I was thrown into and eventually embraced wholeheartedly.

What was the biggest lesson I took from this? Don't stop living. I know I heard the gasps of the newbies in the crowd, but you will thank me for this advice. Be mindful that you are investing years of your time, whether you are caring for your parents at home or not. To avoid burnout, you must take time for yourself and continue with life. Take me for example, I had longed for a vacation with my family but always dreaded leaving in case one of our parents passed while I was away. My mother was on the brink of death more times than I can honestly recall. Yet, each time I tried to leave, the guilt and anxiety would riddle me. I began to notice the pattern of my mother's health. We would be alerted to her last moments just to watch her bounce back more than a dozen times.

After a discussion with my brother, we agreed that we both had to move forward. We laid out concession plans in case something were to happen. The situation would be handled without me if need be. I took that vacation, and my father passed while I was away, yet I know I was right where he would have wanted me to be. I was able to attend the final planning meeting with my brother remotely. I was even able to attend the funeral service via Zoom. The cruise ship I was on even offered a chapel for me to watch the service. What is the point of all this? There is an answer for it all, you don't have to be there 100% of your time, and chances are, your parents would want you to continue to strive for joy and happiness in your life. I am a parent, and I know that is what I would want.

Once my father was gone, I felt a profound emptiness. My purpose was suddenly ripped away from me. I now had more time, yet I had no idea what to do with it. It was then that I realized I had been so wrapped up in the lives of my parents that I hadn't given enough thought to my future.

It was an arduous process to pick myself up, but I knew I had to do it. There's no rulebook for this, no clear path to tread. It's about rediscovering yourself and remembering that you are not just a caregiver but also a person with dreams and aspirations.

Taking care of my health was my priority. Years of caring for others had taken a toll on my mental and physical well-being. I started scheduling regular health check-ups, working out, and taking up yoga and meditation. I prioritized my sleep schedule and tried to maintain a balanced diet. It was surprising how much of a difference these small changes made.

Next came the process of rediscovering my interests and passions. It was almost like getting to know myself all over again. I had to redefine who I was outside of being a caregiver. I started doing things I loved–reading, gardening. I traveled to places I'd always wanted to visit but couldn't because of my caregiving duties. I made time for friends and even made new ones.

I also sought out professional help. I found a therapist who specializes in grief counseling. Those sessions gave me a safe space to express my emotions and learn coping mechanisms to deal with my grief. It is difficult, but the effort is worth it.

Financial planning was another key aspect. The financial landscape can drastically change with the loss of loved ones. It's important to evaluate the financial implications and plan accordingly. I enlisted the help of a financial advisor to guide me through the process and set me up for a secure future.

One of the most important things I learned is that it's okay to move on. It's not forgetting about your loved ones but rather honoring their memory by living a fulfilling life. They would not have wanted me to wallow in grief, but to keep going, to find happiness and peace again.

Planning for the future after losing your aging parents is not an easy journey, but it must be undertaken. For all those in similar situations, remember to take care of yourself. Embrace your grief, but don't let it consume you. You've spent so much time caring for others; it's time to care for yourself.

Dealing With Loss and Grief After Caregiving

> *The five stages - denial, anger, bargaining, depression, and acceptance - are a part of the framework that makes up our learning to live with the one we lost. They are tools to help us frame and identify what we may be feeling. But they are not stops on some linear timeline in grief.* — Elisabeth Kubler-Ross

The experience of losing someone you've been caring for, especially someone as close as a parent, can trigger a unique kind of grief. Not only are you grieving the loss of a loved one, but you're also grappling with the end of a significant role in your life. The caregiving role you played can create a vacuum once it's over, intensifying feelings of loss and grief. To manage this, consider the steps I have listed below.

1. Acknowledge Your Grief: It's essential to permit yourself to grieve. It's okay to feel sad, and it's okay to cry. Grieving is a personal process, and it might not look the same for everyone. You might experience waves of sadness or a continuous sense of loss. Some days will be harder than others. For example, you might be going about your day when something as simple as your parent(s) favorite song plays on the radio, and it brings a fresh wave of grief. It's okay. Allow yourself to feel these emotions fully. Although painful, this is normal.

2. Seek Support: After your loved one's death, you may feel incredibly alone, especially since your role as a caregiver likely consumed a lot of your time and energy. Reach out to friends, family, or support groups for individuals who have lost a loved one. People who have experienced similar losses can provide empathy and advice. An example of this could be joining a local or online grief support group, where you can share your experiences and feelings with others who are going through the same thing.

3. Honor Your Loved One: Find ways to remember and honor your loved one. This could be as simple as lighting a candle in his memory, creating a photo album, or planting a tree in their name. For example, if your parent(s) had a favorite park, you could sponsor a bench in their name or participate in events that were important to them. These acts not only honor your loved one, but they can also help you work through your grief.

4. Practice Self-Care: Caregiving often involves putting the needs of others before your own. Now, it's important to take time to care for yourself. This can include activities like eating healthy meals, getting regular exercise, or pursuing hobbies that you enjoy and find comforting. An example of self-care is starting a daily meditation or yoga practice to manage stress and foster inner peace.

Coping With Guilt After Caregiving

Guilt is a common emotion for caregivers after a loved one dies. You may feel guilty for not doing more, not doing enough, or simply for surviving. I wanted to include ways to cope with these feelings.

Guilt Is a Normal Part of Grief: Guilt is a common reaction to loss. It's normal to wish that you could have done more or that things could have been different. We may spiral into the space of "I didn't get to say goodbye" or "I hope they knew how much I loved them." Acknowledge these feelings and remember this is all normal. The important part is to let it out in whatever way works for you. There will be those who are content lighting a candle; others may need to go ax throwing or smash plates. Again, this is your unique grief journey.

Forgive Yourself: It's easy to fixate on your perceived shortcomings as a caregiver. However, you must remember that you did your best given the circumstances. Try to forgive yourself for any mistakes or regrets. I doubt we could find even one person coming out of caregiving who believes they did a perfect job. That is a fantasy. You showed up, and that is enough. It is time to let all the rest of that shit go.

If you are truly struggling with the guilt, you could consider writing a letter to your parent(s) expressing your feelings of guilt and asking for forgiveness. This can be a powerful step in processing your feelings and beginning to forgive yourself.

Seek Professional Help: If feelings of guilt become overwhelming, it may be helpful to seek professional help, like a therapist or counselor. They can provide tools and strategies to cope with guilt and grief healthily. For example, a grief counselor might recommend a technique called cognitive reframing, where you learn to identify and challenge negative thought patterns, turning them into positive ones. So, in those moments of feeling you didn't do enough, you would reframe that to say, "I am enough, and I gave all I could."

Celebrate Your Caregiving: You were there for your parents when they needed you most. This is something to be proud of. Celebrate your caregiving journey and the love and dedication it demonstrated.

Grief and guilt are normal parts of the healing process. They're signs of love and connection. By understanding and working through these emotions, you can start to find peace and healing after your loss. It takes time and patience, so remember to be gentle with yourself as you navigate this difficult journey.

Rebuilding Your Life After Caregiving

The passing of a parent is a significant event, and the transition from being a caregiver to redefining your life after they are gone can be challenging. It is very normal to grieve the ones we are caring for long before they pass. We miss who they were before they got sick. I have included some suggestions to guide you through this transition:

- **Allow yourself to grieve:** This is a profound loss, and you permit yourself permission to experience the grief your way and at your pace. Don't rush the process. It's okay to cry, to be angry, or to feel numb.
- **Lean on your strengths:** Each individual copes with loss in their unique way, but the abilities acquired as a caregiver can be of benefit. The passing of your loved one doesn't diminish your core qualities. You continue to possess compassion, devotion, dedication, resilience, determination, adaptability, perseverance, intelligence, bravery, and a sense of humor. These attributes will remain with you as you progress through this next phase.
- **Seek emotional support:** Reach out to friends, family, or professional counselors to share your feelings and experiences. If you feel comfortable, consider joining a support group for people who have gone through similar experiences. These groups can change our

perspective through the views of others who have been in our shoes. We can see that there is life after caregiving.

- **Physical health:** We know all too well how much focus has been taken from you and your health. Now is the time to take care of your physical health. Regular exercise, healthy eating, and getting enough sleep are vital during stress and grief.
- **Return to (or find) your passions:** Perhaps there were hobbies or interests you set aside while caregiving. Now might be the time to return to those activities. Or, try new hobbies that you have always been interested in but never had time for.
- **Take time for yourself:** You've likely spent time focused on the needs of another person. It's okay now to focus on yourself and what you want and need. This could be as simple as taking a relaxing bath, reading a book, or going for a quiet walk.
- **Plan for the future:** Reflect on what you want your life to look like moving forward. This could involve setting new career goals, planning travels, or considering where you'd like to live. You may also consider seeking guidance from a life coach or a counselor to assist in this planning.
- **Consider volunteering or working:** You may consider getting a job, going back to work, or

volunteering. This can provide structure to your day, an opportunity to socialize, and a sense of purpose.

Be mindful that rebuilding your life after such a significant event should be taken slowly. Just because someone in your support group is rebounding into a blissful life after just three weeks does not mean you must follow. Take the time you need. It's okay to ask for help, and it's okay to have days when you don't feel like you're making progress. Be patient with yourself and take one day at a time.

> *Grief is real because loss is real. Each grief has its own imprint, as distinctive and as unique as the person we lost. The pain of loss is so intense, so heartbreaking, because in loving we deeply connect with another human being, and grief is the reflection of the connection that has been lost. We think we want to avoid the grief, but really it is the pain of the loss we want to avoid. Grief is the healing process that ultimately brings us comfort in our pain.*
>
> — Elisabeth Kubler-Ross

As I walked into the sunset of this phase, I carried the love and memories of my parents as they once were, not as a burden but as a beacon of light guiding me through the uncharted territories of life post-caregiving. I learned to embrace the solitude and the silence, seeing these as not just reminders of loss but as symbols of peace, spaces within which I could reflect, grow, and continue to love my father in his absence. His spirit, his laughter, his lessons—all live on in me, giving me the strength to move forward, to explore and rediscover my own identity beyond caregiving.

As I pen down these final lines of this chapter, I am more than a daughter who lost her father and has a mother with dementia; I am a survivor navigating her way through the labyrinth of life and loss. I am a testament to the transformative power of love and the resilience of the human spirit. Moving on from caregiving has not been a departure from my parents but a journey toward myself. I am the woman my parents raised, the caregiver they entrusted with their twilight years, and the survivor they knew I would become. My father may no longer be physically present, and my mom may be cognitively absent, but they continue to live within me, their lives a continuous song that I sing with every step I take into the future.

Afterword

As I draw the final strokes of my pen on this narrative, I am struck by a profound sense of humility and gratitude. Not for the experiences that led me to author this book—no one would wish such trials on their worst enemy—but for the opportunity to share my journey, to bear witness to the struggles and the triumphs of the sandwich generation, and perhaps most importantly, to offer some tangible, actionable support to those who find themselves in the same predicament.

As a teacher, I was accustomed to making learning an enjoyable process, but nothing prepared me for the lessons life had in store for me as I stepped into the role of a caregiver for my aging parents. The walls of my classroom became the confining walls of my home. The young faces I mentored each day were replaced with the familiar, albeit fading, expressions of my parents.

Home safety was no longer about ensuring the furniture corners were padded for my kids but about installing grab

Afterword

bars in the bathroom, removing tripping hazards, and ensuring my parents could navigate their home with ease. Legal and financial matters became a labyrinth that required more than a classroom education, as I had to familiarize myself with wills, power of attorney, and the maze of healthcare insurance.

Siblings, once partners in crime during our childhood, transformed into fellow soldiers on the caregiving battlefield. Our shared responsibility occasionally led to conflicts, forcing us to learn and master the art of patient communication and compromise. The pressure and strain of balancing work and caregiving presented their own unique challenges, compelling me to seek solutions in flexible working arrangements, empathy from colleagues, and, most importantly, self-care.

Finally, the toughest lesson yet was in accepting and planning for a future when my caregiving journey would end. The inevitability of loss forced me to face my own mortality and ponder over the legacy I would leave behind. Yet, this contemplation brought with it a certain peace as it shed light on the importance of cherishing every moment.

As I stand on the threshold of the future, looking back, the sorrow and struggle are there, but they do not define my experience. Instead, it's the moments of connection, the shared laughter, the wisdom gleaned from my parents' stories, and the opportunity to truly give back to those who gave me a life that paints a richer, more vibrant picture.

The journey of caregiving, with all its trials and triumphs, was a chance to truly live the circle of life. It brought perspective, understanding, patience, strength, and, most importantly, immense love. To anyone walking a similar

Afterword

path, know that you are not alone. Your struggles are shared, and your triumphs are celebrated.

As this book closes, my wish is that these words be a beacon for those traveling the caregiving path. This journey, marked by both tears and joy, serves as a testament that we endure, we adapt, we love, and in doing so, we discover a strength within ourselves we never knew we possessed.

It is true that caregiving often feels like a storm you're weathering, but remember, every storm passes. Eventually, the sun does shine, revealing a transformed landscape touched by the storm but standing resilient. In the heart of every caregiver is the sun, a beacon of light and love, always ready to shine, no matter how heavy the clouds. May we all find the strength to keep our light burning bright. After all, it's not just about enduring but living and loving through the storm.

I started this book amidst a storm of confusion and heartbreak. I was a teacher—a nurturer, but I found myself at a loss as I watched my parents gradually fade into the mists of dementia. My father has since passed, leaving a void no words can fill, and my mother continues to battle the relentless tide of her illness. And yet, I end this book with a heart brimming with gratitude.

The journey I embarked on has been a life-changing one, marked by trials, tribulations, and tears. But it has also been a journey of love, resilience, and unanticipated growth. Amidst the sorrow, I have found pockets of joy—moments of clarity from my mother that are more precious than any gem, shared laughter with my siblings that echo with the innocence of our childhood, and a newfound appreciation for the fleeting beauty of life.

Afterword

To all who are currently in the role of caregiver, I see you–you are not alone. I hear you and all the frustrations you are facing–you are not alone. I feel you, and all the times you feel completely alone or incapable–you are not alone. As I journey into the next phase of caregiving, rebuilding my life, I want to tell you just how brave and courageous you are.

 Calling all compassionate souls and dedicated caregivers!

Have you ever finished a book and thought, "Wow, this really impacted my life"? Well, I've got an exciting proposition for you today! By leaving a review for this book, you can not only help others but also experience a profound sense of fulfillment. Allow me to explain.

Think about this: how amazing does it feel when you're able to lend a helping hand to someone in need? Whether it's a small act of kindness or a grand gesture, the act of helping others fills our hearts with joy and purpose. So, here's your chance to make a difference in someone else's life and pay it forward.

Leaving a review for this book is an opportunity for you to deliver value to others during what may be a difficult time. By sharing your honest thoughts, insights, and personal takeaways, you're offering valuable guidance to fellow readers who may be going through the challenging journey of caring for their aging parents. Your words have the power to uplift, inspire, and bring hope to those who need it most.

Now, you might be wondering, why does this book need your review? Well, my dear reader, the answer lies in the transformative effect it can have on the lives of others. Your review will serve as a beacon of light, helping those who are feeling lost, overwhelmed, or unsure of how to navigate the complexities of caring for their aging loved one. Your words can provide

Afterword

solace, practical advice, and the reassurance that they are not alone on this challenging path.

So, here's the big ask: Could you spare a few moments to leave an honest review for this book? Your feedback is so valuable in spreading awareness about this guide and helping it to reach those who need it the most.

Leaving a review is as easy as pie! Simply head over to Amazon or Goodreads and find the book's page. Once there, click on the "Write a Review" button, pour your heart out about the impact this book had on you, and hit that submit button. Easy peasy, right? Or just scan the QR to take you right to the review page.

Scan the QR CODE to go directly to Amazon to review

Your review has the power to make a positive impact on others. By sharing your experience, you can guide someone else through the challenges, helping them regain their sanity, find peace of mind, and restore life balance. Your words can be a lifeline for someone who desperately needs it.

As an extra little motivation, imagine introducing this valuable resource to someone who is struggling with caring for their aging loved one. By leaving a review, you're not only helping them but also opening doors to goodwill from other compassionate souls who are eager to lend support and share their own experiences.

So, I thank you for reading my book. I hope it is a helpful resource. Now let's come together and make a difference in the lives of others. Leave your

Afterword

honest review for "Caring for Aging Parents" today, and let's create a community of support and understanding. Together, we can navigate the challenges of caring for our loved ones and find strength in unity. It's the reason I wrote this book in the first place.

Keep shining your light bright!

Scan the QR CODE to go directly to Amazon to review

Glossary

All terms and definitions are sourced from (AARP, 2021)

Activities of daily living (ADLs): Routine activities that people do every day without needing assistance, including eating, bathing, dressing, toileting, transferring, and continence.

Acute care: Medical care is provided for a short duration to treat a specific illness or condition. These can include brief hospital stays, doctor visits, or surgery.

Adult care home: Also referred to as an adult family-care home (AFCH) or a group home. An assisted living home where qualified staff supports disabled adults or seniors who need assistance with daily tasks but want to remain independent.

Adult daycare: These centers offer companionship and aid to older adults who need are not able to be left alone

Glossary

for safety reasons during the day. The programs can help give a break to a round-the-clock caregiver.

Advance directives: Written statements that portray individuals' medical choices if they become unable to make their own decisions.

Aging in Place: A term used to describe a person living in the residence of their choice, for as long as they are able, as they age.

Alzheimer's Disease: A progressive brain disorder that impairs memory, thinking, and behavior, and is the most common cause of dementia among older adults.

Assisted living: A long-term care option that combines housing, support services, and health care, as needed.

Assistive technology devices: These products are designed to help a person's ability to live and function independently. On the low end of the technology devices, we see canes and pill organizers; on the high end of tech, we see items like electric wheelchairs, smartphones, and hearing aids.

Caregiver burnout: A state of physical, emotional, and mental exhaustion that can occur when caregivers don't get the help they need or if they try to do more than they are able to.

Care plan: A strategy for managing a person's healthcare needs, typically created by a healthcare professional.

Cardiologist: A medical specialist who cares for and diagnoses issues of the heart.

Chronic diseases: A medical condition that persists

past one year and demands ongoing medical intervention or limits an individual's ability to care for themselves.

Cognitive Decline: A decrease in cognitive abilities such as memory and thinking skills.

Companion Care: Non-medical care, supervision, and socialization services provided to a senior or disabled person.

Competence: When we discuss the legality of competence, we need to review the individual and their ability to comprehend information, make decisions based on that information, and discuss their decision in a comprehensive way.

Conservator: The courts may appoint an individual to take care of the finances of a person that cannot handle the job any longer.

Continence: The ability of an individual to control their bladder and bowel function.

Copayment: Also referred to as copays. These are set amounts—$30, for example—that a person pays for a medical service that is covered by insurance after paying the deductible. For example, your health plan's billable cost for a medical appointment is $120. Not meeting the deductible for the year, you'll need to pay the full $120. If you have met your deductible, you pay the $20 copay.

Delirium: When an individual shows signs of short-term confusion, cognition, and disrupted attention followed by confusing speech and hallucinations.

Dementia: An overall term for diseases and conditions characterized by a decline in memory, language, problem-

Glossary

solving, and other thinking skills that affect a person's ability to perform everyday activities.

Dependent: An individual who relies on another for support, often financially, physically, or emotionally.

Dermatologist: A medical specialist who treats skin-related issues.

Do not resuscitate (DNR) order: This is a directive put in place by a person who has no measures taken to save their life. This includes not attempting to restart the heart if the heart or breathing stops.

Elder abuse: Harm inflicted upon an older adult, which can take the form of physical, emotional, sexual abuse, financial exploitation, or neglect.

End-of-life doula: Also referred to as a death doula. A person who offers non-medical comfort and support to someone who is dying. They address both the person and their family. They offer education and guidance as well as emotional, spiritual, or practical care.

Geriatric care manager: A health and human services specialist who helps families care for older relatives while encouraging as much independence as possible.

Geriatrician: A physician who specializes in the care of older adults, focusing on the health care needs of people who are aged 65 and older.

Gastroenterologist: A medical person who is trained and specializes in issues of the gut and digestive disorders.

Guardianship: Legal process designed to protect vulnerable individuals who are unable to care for themselves by appointing a guardian.

Glossary

Healthcare proxy: Grants a healthcare person or an attorney to be a spokesperson and make medical decisions for anyone who can no longer communicate or has cognitive decline.

Home health agency: A nonprofit company, certified by Medicare, that offers healthcare services like nursing, personal care, social work, and even occupational, physical, or speech therapy in a patient's home.

Home Modification: Changes made to adapt living spaces to meet the needs of people with physical limitations so that they can continue to live independently and safely.

Hospice care: A type of care for terminally ill patients and their families, providing comfort and palliative care rather than curative treatment.

Incontinence: The loss of control over urination and/or defecation.

Informed consent: Making decisions regarding a person's medical care with full disclosure. This means honest communication with the patient, and entire family, and the healthcare team. Everyone is informed and on the same page.

Life Alert: A home emergency response system aimed at ensuring the safety of seniors living alone, providing immediate medical help at the press of a button.

Living will: A document outlining the wishes, regarding the types of medical treatment you want as you approach. These are enforced when the person is unable to speak for themselves.

Long-term care insurance: Insurance designed to cover the costs of long-term care services, including services in your home and care in a variety of facility and community settings.

Long-term care ombudsman: This person is an advocate for residents of nursing homes, residential care homes, and assisted living homes. They are trained in conflict resolution; they give information on how to locate a facility and how to ensure the best care.

Medicare: A federal program that provides health insurance to people 65 years of age or older, certain younger individuals with disabilities, and people with End-Stage Renal Disease.

Memory care: A type of senior living or specialized care specifically designed for people with Alzheimer's disease, dementia, and other types of memory problems.

Mild cognitive impairment (MCI): An intermediate stage between the expected cognitive decline of normal aging and the more serious decline of dementia.

Neurologist: A physician specializing in neurology and trained to investigate, diagnose, and treat neurological disorders.

Occupational Therapy: Therapy designed to help individuals perform daily living activities, particularly after a health crisis.

Oncologist: A medical doctor who has specialized in the world of cancer.

Palliative care: Specialized medical care for people with serious illnesses, focusing on providing relief from symptoms and stress.

Patient advocate: A professional who can resolve

concerns about someone's health care experience, particularly problems that cannot be taken care of immediately.

Power of attorney: A legal document that gives one person the authority to act for another person in specified or all legal or financial matters.

Primary care physician (PCP): Your main doctor you see for checkups and health issues. These professionals often have family practices for all ages, but some specialize in internal medicine for adults only.

Progressive disease: A disease or disorder that continues to worsen over time

Psychiatrist: A medical professional who specializes in emotional and mental concerns, disorders, or issues.

Psychologist: Not a medical doctor, but a specialist who can discuss with patients and families emotional and personal issues and help them make decisions.

Remote patient monitoring (RPM): A category of telehealth services that enables patients to use mobile medical technology to get patient-generated health data, like weight, blood pressure, and heart rate, and then send it to a healthcare professional.

Respite care: Temporary relief for caregivers, providing a short period of rest or relief from caregiving responsibilities.

Rheumatologist. A doctor who specializes in pain and symptoms related to joints and the musculoskeletal system. This includes bones, ligaments, cartilage, muscles, and tendons.

Sandwich generation: The generation of people

Glossary

who care for their aging parents while supporting their own children.

Senior center: A physical place that provides opportunities for aging adults to be active, enjoy social activities and improve their quality of life. This occurs in a safe location.

Senior housing: Living arrangements designed exclusively for seniors, and vary widely in terms of features, amenities, and services offered.

Skilled nursing facility (SNF): A type of nursing home recognized by the Medicare and Medicaid systems as meeting long-term healthcare needs for individuals who have the potential to function independently after a limited period of care.

Sundowning: A phenomenon associated with increased confusion and restlessness in patients with some form of dementia, most commonly Alzheimer's disease, that usually occurs in the late afternoon or early evening.

Telemedicine: The use of digital communication technologies to access health care services remotely and manage health care.

Urologist. A doctor who specializes in disorders of the male reproductive system and the urinary tract health of both men and women.

Vital signs. Indicates signs of life — a person's heart rate, breathing rate, body temperature, and blood pressure. They give doctors a clear picture of how well a person's body is functioning.

Wandering: A common behavior in individuals with

dementia characterized by aimless walking or traveling around a familiar environment.

References

AARP. (2021, October 27). *Caregiver's glossary for commonly used caregiving terms.* AARP. https://www.aarp.org/caregiving/basics/info-2019/caregiver-glossary.html

Alzheimer's Society. (n.d.). *What is dementia?* Alzheimer Society of Canada. Retrieved June 1, 2023, from https://alzheimer.ca/en/about-dementia/what-dementia?gclid=CjwKCAjwg-GjBhBnEiwAMUvNW7CZgm5Xx1JKLKaunhsje2LzmKsTYQAttXQjhqV1NSu_KRy7FbW63B0COm0QAvD_BwE

The Arbor Company. (2023, April 16). *18 tips for dealing with stubborn, aging parents.* www.arborcompany.com. https://www.arborcompany.com/blog/18-tips-for-dealing-with-stubborn-aging-parents

Baum, J. (2023, January 19). *What is a home safety assessment for the elderly?* EHealth.https://www.ehealthinsurance.com/medicare/blog/medicare-tips/what-is-a-home-safety-assessment-for-the-elderly/

Brain & Life. (2018, January). *How to reclaim life after years of caregiving.* Www.brainandlife.org. https://www.brainandlife.org/articles/reclaiming-life-after-years-of-caregiving-is-a-gradual-up

Cleveland Clinic. (2023, June 1). *Forget me not: What to remember about memory loss.* Cleveland Clinic. https://my.clevelandclinic.org/health/symptoms/11826-memory-loss

Columbia University. (2021, June 10). *Changes that occur to the aging brain: What happens when we get older.* Columbia University's Mailman School of Public Health. https://www.publichealth.columbia.edu/news/changes-occur-aging-brain-what-happens-when-we-get-older

Family Caregiver Alliance. (n.d.). *Caregiver stories.* Family Caregiver Alliance. Retrieved June 20, 2023, from https://www.caregiver.org/connecting-caregivers/caregiver-stories/

Family Caregiver Alliance. (2021, June 4). *Caregiving at home: A guide to community resources.* Family Caregiver Alliance. https://www.caregiver.org/resource/caregiving-home-guide-community-resources/

Geiger, B. (2018, August 12). *What documents should be part of the estate plan if an aging parent becomes unable to make financial or medical*

References

decisions? Geiger Law Office.https://www.geigerlawoffice.com/blog/estate-planning-for-aging-parents.cfm#:~:text=The%20key%20documents%20in%20a

Hager, M. (2019, January 9). *What is A certified aging-in-place specialist and how can they help?* Aging in Place. https://ageinplace.com/aging-in-place-professionals/what-is-an-aging-in-place-specialist-and-how-can-they-help/

Health Hub. (2023, June 16). *MindSG*. Www. health hub. sg. https://www.healthhub.sg/programmes/186/MindSG/Caring-For-Others/My-Elderly-Parent

Hibbs, S. (2017, June 27). *Now what? 10 ways to adjust to life after caregiving*. Cancer.net. https://www.cancer.net/blog/2017-06/now-what-10-ways-adjust-life-after-caregiving

Mayo Clinic. (2021, June 17). *Dementia - symptoms, and causes*. Mayo Clinic. https://www.mayoclinic.org/diseases-conditions/dementia/symptoms-causes/syc-20352013accessible

The Memory Center. (2018, September 28). *12 tips for adjusting to life after being A caregiver*. https://www.thememorycenter.com/taking-care-of-yourself-managing-time-after-being-a-caregiver/

Metropolis. (2021, July 26). *6 common health problems in the elderly and ways to manage them right*. Metropolis Blogs. https://www.metropolisindia.com/blog/health-wellness/common-health-problems-in-elderly-and-ways-to-manage-them-right/

National Institute on Aging. (n.d.) *Aging in place: Tips on making home safe and accessible* https://www.nia.nih.gov/health/infographics/aging-place-tips-making-home-safe-and-accessible

National Institute on Aging. (2023, January 25). *Talking with your older patients*. National Institute on Aging. https://www.nia.nih.gov/health/talking-your-older-patients

Peters, R. (2006). Aging and the brain. *Postgraduate Medical Journal, 82*(964), 84–88. https://doi.org/10.1136/pgmj.2005.036665

Tabar, E. (2020, December 17). *Taking care of elderly parents quotes*. Freedom Care. https://freedomcare.com/taking-care-of-elderly-parents-quotes/

Tesoro-Morioka, M. (n.d.). *Care coordination: How to share caregiving responsibilities with family members - ready set care*. Www.readysetcare.com. Retrieved June 12, 2023, from https://www.readysetcare.com/resources/articles/care-coordination-tips

References

Trovato, J. (2023, January 9). *This home safety checklist for seniors will help you and your loved one's age safely at home.* Health.com. https://www.health.com/home/home-safety-checklist-seniors

Printed in Dunstable, United Kingdom